INDO-PAK RELATIONS
Prospect and Retrospect

Edited by

Joseph Benjamin

Reference Press

4831/24, Ansari Road
Darya Ganj
New Delhi-110 002
Phone : 23260807
Fax : 23274173
E-mail: essess@del3vsnl.net.in

First Published 2004

ISBN : 81-88583-37-5

Price : Rs. 450/-

Published by :

Reference Press

4831/24, Ansari Road, Darya Ganj,
New Delhi - 110 002
Phone : 23260807
Fax : 23274173

Laser Typesetting:

Mukesh Graphics

L-2/8, DDA Market,
Mangolepuri, New Delhi
Ph. : 27924405

Printed at :

Print Line

Contents

Maps

Apendices

Preface

This book is a collection of research papers written by various experts from varied disciplines and professions is edited with discernment covering the wide gamut of bilateral relations inside out. Several issues which not only hogged the media limelight but has given new turn and twists to the turbulent relationship has been given in-depth sophisticated analysis. The topics which competed for inclusion in this editorial offering is Kargil Stand-off, Cross-border terrorism , SAARC , economic and trade linkages , geo-political setting of the conflict and is topped by a historical survey which in themselves gives to any serious reader enough material to mull and ponder over. This includes also serious academicians , policy-makers and students of Indo-Pak Relations who not only shape public opinion but also contribute their invisible input in corridors of power.

The book has seen the light of day due to timely financial support of esteemed national body , India Council of Social Science Research , New Delhi. This facilitated and motivated the department of Political Science , St. Francis de Sales' College , Seminary Hills , Nagpur to organize a National Seminar on the pertinent theme **Indo-Pak Relations** on 7-8, January ,2003. The principal of St. Francis de sales' College, Fr. Anthony D'Souza deserves thanks for being source of inspiration and helping out in possible way to make the National Seminar a big success.

In preparation of this book in its present form I owe debt to many institutions and individuals. Some of them I would like to mention are Mr. Shanker Bose, Deputy Director, and Dr. (Mrs.) Ramesh Madan, Asstt. Director of ICSSR, New Delhi, students of Political Science department, St. Francis de Sales' College in general and Brother Devasahaya in particular.

In the hard and grueling task of editing of the book I have been helped by Prof. John Alexander. At familial level I have been backed up to the hilt by my wife Pratibha and sons Prashant and Jayant who showed unusual patience and forbearance when I was too involved in the work. Last but not the least I am thankful to Rev. Fr. Paulson , OP, whose unstinted cooperation was extended to *me* with a cheerful heart. I thank Mr Virendra Tatode for helping me in typing and computer work.

I acknowledge my heart-felt thanks to Mr. Sumit Sethi , Ess Ess Publisher , New Delhi who has kindly consented to publish this path-breaking book entitled **Indo-Pak Relations :Prospect and Retrospect** as early as possible.

Joseph Benjamin

Head,
Department of Political Science
St. Francis de Sales' College,
Seminary Hills,
Nagpur -440 006
Maharashtra
Dated: May 5,2003.

About the Editor and Contributors

Editor

Dr. Joseph Benjamin has done considerable research on the problems of weaker sections of Indian society. He has published a number of high quality articles in papers and prestigious magazines. His book which is published is "Scheduled Caste in Indian Politics and Society". Currently he is Reader and Head, Department of Political Science, St. Francis de Sales College, (Nagpur University), Nagpur. He is also an Executive Member, Maharashtra Political Science and Public Administration Association.

Contributors

Anand Mavalankar is Professor in the Department of Political Science, M.S University of Baroda, Vadodra, Gujrat.

Vijay Kumar is Professor and Head in the Department of Political Science, T.M. University of Bhagalpur, Bihar.

Ram Dev Bharadwaj is Senior Lecturer in the Department of Political Science, Rani Durgawati University, Jabalpur (M.P).

Mohan Kashikar is Reader in the Department of Political Science, Nagpur University Nagpur.

Indra Mohan Jha is Lecturer in the Department Political Science, A.R.S.D College, (University of Delhi) Delhi.

John Alexander is a well known historian. He has retired as Head of the Department of History from St. Francis de Sales College (Nagpur University), Nagpur.

Jayant Umranikar is an IPS and currently he is Addl. Director General and Commissioner of Police, Nagpur. He was in Pakistan for four years on deputation.

Nalini Kant Jha is the Dean and Professor in School of International Studies. Pondicherry University, Pondicherry.

1
Introduction

Joseph Benjamin

Quite often relationships between any two countries is assumed to remain cordial and harmonious. But when we witness relationship between the two neighbouring countries i.e., India and Pakistan , it is conflictual. This synchronizes with the time of partition when both the dominions were granted independence by the departing British authority in the sub-continent. The traumatic event of partition was caused by deep-seated religious antagonism between the two communities i.e., Hindus and Muslims. It may be added that when the Muslims League's leader Mohammad Ali Jinnah staked the claim for an independent Muslim state ,there was a section of Muslim community who differed from him and opted to remain in India. After granting independence to India and Pakistan ,the British Government did not fully sever its links , but retained benevolent interest in the affairs of the sub-continent . Pakistan anti-India foreign policy which was also a product of its domestic politics compulsion since 1947 waged full-fledged conventional wars and assorted mini skirmishes across the LOC . So it had both overt and covert dimensions . The tribal invasion was an example of brutal intrusion just couple of months after independence.

The ruling elite of Pakistan unfortunately enough never

believed in the policy of cooperation and co-existence with India. Pakistan suffered from an obsession to remain always in terms of parity with its neighbour .Whether it is economic development , social progress or military capability the competitive urge remained paramount in the psyche of movers and shakers of Pakistan. In realization of this tall order for a country smaller in size , population and resources, the overdrive is remarkable. It turned to every conceivable foreign source for beefing up its military strength , economic development despite favouable or unfavouable currents and cross-currents of international politics. It leaned on both capitalist USA , Communist China and others with cool calculation and well honed self- interest .And it also turned to West Asian petro-dollar rich Muslim countries for money for its economy and for making of an Islamic Bomb.

Thus parameters of Islamabad's foreign policy foredoomed any conciliatory gestures towards its neigbhour ,as it was more focused on acquiring influence , prestige and clout in South Asia and in world affairs. The attitude of a wide cross-sections of Pakistani society suffers from a pathological hatred towards India and Indians. In this context , even if Kashmir dispute is solved favourable to Pakistan's wishes , it remains a moot question whether it would bring much sought amity between the two countries. The pre and post-partition memories have seared the minds of many people in both the countries, which becomes a veritable stumbling-block to open a new bright chapter in friendly relationship. Bordering on the margin of triviality one would speculate that had India remained united as one geographical unit , perhaps this bitterness between the two nations may not have been there in the very first place. India was divided on the basis of religion but secession of Bangladesh from Pakistan exploded the notion of two-nation theory.

Religion cannot be the all effective glue which can cement and bind people for long. Culture ,geography , economics, social cohesiveness and other variables keeps the people together. Many scholars and thinkers have opined that the geographical land mass which comprises India, Pakistan and Bangladesh today has a deep underlying cultural unity. Unfortunately some ideologues and proponents of a separate homeland for Muslims were carried away so much with their strongly held belief that they were not averse to division of the subcontinent. In this category were men like Mohammad Iqbal, Mohammad Ali Jinnah etc. The inevitable corollary of this mind-set and world view meant that the leaders of Pakistan always looked to India with jaundiced eyes. Keith Callard, a well known Canadian writer who insightfully observes: "It would be quite right to suggest that the feeling of the Pakistani towards India is one of simple hatred. Their attitude is rather one of intense rivalry to the point of bitter jealously."

Zulfikar Ali Bhutto the charismatic yet inveterate India-baiter as Foreign Minister had observed: " We are fully aware of the treacherous nature of India and we do not want to endanger the existence of Pakistan in the name of cooperation." He in his book *The Myth of Independence* also stated that "The people of Pakistan want relations with India without entanglement. Confrontation which means neither peace nor war must be continued as a measure of self-defence until India realizes the need to settle all disputes with Pakistan on the basis of recognized international merit and in a spirit equality... It may be said that only way out of a clash of conflicting interest will a final synthesis be found in Asia and with it a tolerable peace. A long and arduous road has to be covered from confrontation to cooperation ,"

An attempt was made to study and understand the dynamics of the Indo-Pak relations through a National Seminar on Indo-Pak Relations which was organized under the auspices of the Department of Political Science , St. Francis de Sales' College , Nagpur on 7-8 January 2003. The present book is the outcome of National Seminar on Indo-Pak relations. Many esteemed scholars and intellectuals were the resource persons.

Prof. John Alexander's paper concentrate on the genesis of

Indo-Pak Relations since 1947. As one who has studied history, he has brought into sharper focus the factors leading to partition and its aftermath. This enables one to understand the confrontational relationship between two warring neighbouring countries. The relationship between India and Pakistan has been turbulent and stormy , with few occasional patches of cooperation. In his paper an attempt is made to study in-depth the Indo-Pak Relations since independence. After 1947 , Kashmir remained as a thorn in the flesh, and to Islamabad it was the unfinished agenda of partition. The rulers of Pakistan did not desist from using force to grab Jammu and Kashmir. They have already used force several times on the battle field to grab Kashmir.

Pandit Jawaharlal Nehru ,the first Prime Minister of independent India ,caught up in the swirling waters of fast emerging Kashmir imbroglio , had the support of the then Dorga ruler Hari Singh and also the backing of Sheikh Abdullah , influential leader of the National Conference. Once the Instrument of Accession was signed by Hari Singh ,the Hindu ruler , then the Government of India's position became strong legally and it sent military force to checkmate the designs of the tribal invaders and Pakistan army. From the very start of their independent existence both the new nations were locked up in simmering conflict, which took at times shape of wars and at times was nothing short of low-intensity proxy war. In his paper, one caveat also figured in prominently that nations which were in conflict for centuries like France versus Germany, Britain versus France decided wisely enough to bury the hatchet for good. However, it is always a matter of long haul and resolution of Indo- Pak conflict in any near future is no exception to this aside. Another illustrative historical example which could be a source of enlightenment for ruling elites of both nations is US-Canada relationship. They share a long unguarded border and enjoy perfect harmony except for some momentary hiccups.

The bottom line remains that if India and Pakistan has to enjoy normal friendly relations between themselves, they have to work hard towards it . It is neither authentic history nor far-sighted statesmanship , when one passes on the buck for their continuous acrimony at the door of other nations or individuals.

Indra Mohan Jha, a well known scholar in the field of International Relations in his paper entitled ***Indo-Pak Relations: Lessons in Cooperation*** says that at the root of the Indo-Pak conflict lies the ideological divide between the proponents and opponents of the two-nation theory. India was divided on Hindu-Muslim religious affiliation. The Hindus were not in a favour of partition of the country and the creation of Pakistan. In order to protect the interest of Muslims, the leaders of Muslim League wanted partition . But the tragedy is that the Muslim living in India demography-wise is larger than in the state of Pakistan. They are given same treatment as Hindu citizens in the eyes of law. They participate in the decision-making process of the country. Dr. Zakir Hussain ,the ex-President of India once rightly said, " The Indian Muslim have for the first time in the history been placed in the position of being *co-rulers* in the secular democracy , instead of being the rulers or the ruled." Indra Mohan Jha further said that the two-nation theory continues to embitter relationship between India and Pakistan. There is a ray of hope to make relationship more cordial through policies of cooperation and co-existence. He emphasized that leaders of both the countries get inspiration and enlightenment from the two agreements Indus Water Treaty and Rann of Kutch as there is more scope for similar agreements in different fields of Indo-Pak relations. He finally believes that enduring peace and relationship of friendship can be established between two geographically proximate neighbours through the medium of mutual cooperation.

Anand P Mavalankar in his paper **Indo-Pak Trade and Economic Relations** has studied the bilateral relationship from economic and trade perspective. So far, one has shied away delving deep into the intricacies of economic dimension of the relationship. So, Anand Mavalankar in fitness of things fills in the lacuna. His pointed observation is that during the British Raj in undivided Indian sub-continent exchange of goods and services within the country was quite substantial. The partition of India in 1947 into two independent constituents units and after 1971 which became three units , unfortunately enough left a residue of biases on the basis of religion so the cultural baggage served as an impediment to growth of trade and commerce between the three units. The over all situation became more complex when the two neighbours India and Pakistan due to constraints of foreign policy goals during the period of cold war and post- cold war gravitated towards big powers on ideological, geo-strategic and economic grounds.

To substantiate his analytical premises Anand Mavalankar has given statistical data which leads him to say that "despite noticing an increase in bilateral trade in the 1990s ,official bilateral trade in actual terms was merely Rs. 702 crores for the period 1999-2000." (see in his paper page 78) He envisages that if trade and commercial links has to be cemented well then both New Delhi and Islamabad has to remove all bottlenecks which impedes free flow of goods and services to and fro through all means of communication i.e., road , rail, and sea. Further in his own words "Trade by road between the two countries through Wagha border should be facilitated by mutually agreed procedures of conducting such trade relations." Certain flawed procedures can be abolished in phased manner like the anachronistic one which enjoins that "Ship from Mumbai cannot empty its goods unless it has touched a third country 's port ." Other procedures and impediments can be streamlined in the context of changed international economic environment and national goals of high rate of economic growth .

Jayant Umranikar in his paper on the theme "Indo–Pak Strained Relations" observes the the history of Indo-Pak conflict is similar to a story of two brothers, who had to separate because of the family feud over ancestral property .Pakistan came into existence on August 14,1947 and subsequent relations between the two got acrimonious very soon on the question of Kashmir. Early in 1948 when Indo-Pakistan relations were bitter New Delhi made a large hearted gesture of paying to Pakistan Rs 550 million as her share of the cash balances of undivided India accumulated during the long period of British Raj.

The esteemed IPS officer turned writer of repute was in Pakistan for four years on Government of India deputation .He has sprinkled nuggets of wisdom and insights culled from his experiences over there. He has thrown light about the role of Pakistani political structure, in which the respective status and powers of army , bureaucracy and feudal lords owning large state has been deftly delineated. Plus the judiciary and ubiquitous role of Inter-State Intelligence(ISI) and perennial power struggle amongst them are other factors to be reckored with. They all have weightage and leverage in management of domestic and foreign policy.

He has reached the following conclusion in his own inimitable words "the strained Indo-Pak Relations arise out of the clash of two opposite politico-religious system and divergent societies." And it spills-over into the vexed problem of Jammu and Kashmir which is at the root of Indo-Pak antagonism. His parting punch is "Kashmir is only a symptom but the disease is an inherently flawed relationship."

Ram Dev Bharadwaj casts his gaze intensely on contemporary world's greatest menace Terrorism. The title of his paper is very apt one "Proxy war : In the Shadow of Indo-Pak Relations". His pivotal point is that Pakistan is epicenter of Islamic fundamentalism, conduit point of narco-trafficking and illicit trade in small arms to boot. The powerful nexus between the mullahs , the army ,the bureaucracy and feudal lords has resulted in their sharing political power and privileges between themselves. Because of this the tender plant of Democracy neither could strike root nor thrive in the resultant uncongenial political environment .

As there is no representative government based on a constitution or even if a patchwork constitution is cobbled up ,the governing authority composed of army, bureaucracy and feudal elements have always displayed implacable hostility towards its immediate neighbour India. The unremitting hostility inevitably leads to tensions which at times assumes the nature of full-fledged wars.

The centerpiece of the paper is hinged around the low-key cross-border terrorism which blows hot and cold and is fleshed out in Jammu and Kashmir , which finds its nodal point in Kargil war of 1999 . In contrast Islamabad in the open direct wars of 1947-48, 1965 and 1971 made all out effort to grab Kashmir , though it had been in the shadow of *Jihad* . Be that as it may in the low-intensity proxy war focused on Jammu and Kashmir has been waged by innumerable terrorist outfits which on their own steam or with the backing of ISI has masterminded various terrorist attacks on members of both the communities Hindus and Muslims. So the dividing line between combatants is blurred.

For carrying out their suicidal mission through infiltration, terrorists encompassing many nationalities have been trained in different uses of all sorts of firearms in training camps or selected sites in POK and elsewhere under the watchful eyes and supervision of ISI . The character of terrorism has undergone changes ,as it has become global. Therefore, *Jihadis* of all hues and colour seething with religious fervor have networked well to raise finance , stockpile weapons and to coordinate their strategy to attack their well chosen targets. The watershed event of September 11,2001 when the terrorists struck at World Trade Center ,New York made USA launch a war against terrorism in Afghanistan to flush out Osama bin-Laden ,leader of Al-Qaeda group and Taliban in Afghanistan roping in Pakistan as front-line close ally. War against Afghanistan by USA despite Washington's promises to New Delhi did not dampen either the spirit of terrorists or Pakistan government in stoking the flames of terrorism in Jammu and Kashmir.

Study of Indo-Pak relationship is incomplete if economic dimension is eschewed . Mohan Kashikar fills this gap through his paper ***SAARC and Indo-Pak Relations***. At the very outset, the framers of the SAARC charter has wisely enjoined that there should not be any intermingling of bilateral disputes in multilateral set-up which envisages economic growth and social well-being of all. The strained relations between India and Pakistan have always affected the dynamic functioning of SAARC. The postponement of 11th SAARC summit at Kathmandu and the present stand-off between India and Pakistan has once again stalled the 12th SAARC meet .The proposed summit was scheduled to meet at Islamabad but was torpedoed due to Kashmir dispute centering around cross-border terrorism .Prime Minister Atal Behari Vajpayee said in the press conference on December 11,2002 that "what is the use of going to Pakistan for SAARC meeting when Islamabad is not prepared to talk on any issue expect Kashmir."

Mohan Kashikar after giving a meaningful survey of Indo-Pak relations traces the working and impact of SAARC on the tone and tenor of relationship in recent past.

Dr. Joseph Benjamin in his paper entitled ***Kargil War*** has given a magisterial survey and blow to blow account of the progress of the war , plus the sideward glance to the topography of the geographical terrain and human casualties. He added that the war cloud burst with seismic impact soon after the sweet pleasantries were exchanged between the Indian Prime Minister Atal Behari Vajpayee and his counterpart Prime Miniter Nawaz Sharif . The high hopes generated by the Lahore Declaration were buried deep into the rocky snake pit of mountain heights of Kargil. But after every night there is dawn-likewise Indo-Pak relations can turn a new leaf.

Nalini Kant Jha in his entitled ***India and Pakistan : Prospects for Peace*** observes that there is a hope for peace between the two warring proximate neighbours. He adds that confidence-building measures which has enormous symbolic meaning and message like the reposting of High Commissioners in Islamabad and vice-versa and resumption of air links to and fro would set the stage for authentic resolution of all confluctual issues. Paradoxical though it may appear efforts to forge peace has to be equally matched with military preparedness to fight an inadvertent or accidental war. As international or national politics never remains frozen or unchanged it is argued that any favourable change in both arenas should be optimally harnessed for creation of peaceful bilateral amity. This would also make Islamabad realize the high political economic and social cost to its state and society by maintaining intransigent hostile attitude to India. His recipe is implementation of three pronged strategy i.e., defence preparedness, continued mobilization of international politico-diplomatic support and winning back the goodwill and friendship of Kashmiri people which would give enough elbow-room to policy-makers of New Delhi to take the stream out of Islamabad hostility.

In this present edited book an attempt is made to study Indo-Pak relations form different perspectives . It would be certainly beneficial to the common reader and research scholar alike to comprehend the nuances and shades of none too friendly relationship between the two neighbours who share common past and memories. The contributors in this slim volume belong to different walks of life such as Police Commissioner ,Historian and Political Scientists hailing from different parts of India . Serious research scholars who wishes to have a good peek into the crucible of Indo-Pak relationship , would find the collection a storehouse of vital facts, information larded with insights and under girded by statistics.

It can be said with humility that for the first time a serious effort is being made to include many significant issues i.e., Indo-Pak relations , role of SAARC , cross- border terrorism , Kargil war , Indo-Pak wars , Indo-Pak trade relations in the book. Though one may add , that the cloud of war has not receded from the horizon of the sub-continent despite fond hopes of many –political leaders and lay public of both the nations .

The world scenario and the drumbeats of war which one hears in the wake of simmering conflict in West Asia and US -led coalition's war on Iraq presages new danger inching its way closer to South Asia. The rampaging thrust of globalization under the WTO umbrella and new found US aggressive postures fructifying in unilateralist policy and resort to doctrine of pre-emption must give a wake-up call to ruling elites and general population of both the nations for initiating new breakthroughs to settle bilateral disputes in spirit of dialogue. The road map is Shimla Agreement which precludes third party mediation or intervention .

The bottom line in the final upshot remains that the strategy of dialogue and conciliation should be pursued in a determined way without being disheartened and disillusioned by setbacks and pitfalls coming in the way.

2

INDO-PAK RELATIONS
Post-Independence Relations Perspective

John Alexander

Indo-Pakistani relationship during the last fifty-five years has been turbulent and stormy, with few occasional patches of cooperation. The 'moth-eaten' Pakistan, the land of pure was carved out of undivided India by the departing British due to Hindi-Muslim divisions and long standing estrangement. Hindus, Sikhs and Christians formed minority groups on the newly carved independent state, but the ethnic cleansing of the 1950's and subsequent years have seen their number dwindling.

However, a sizeable Muslim population decided to stay in India. The two nation theory on which platform the Muslim League championed the cause of a new state spearheaded by Mohammed Ali Jinnah the sole spokesman of great intellect and lawyers shrewd sense of timing fought both the British government based in New Delhi and White hall in Britain and the congress party and other parties in fulfillment of the goal.

PRE-PARTITION LEGACY

The British incumbent Home Secretary Jack Straw has acknowledged that the way the British left India left some problems, because the partition and granting of independence was done in sloppy way with great haste. Three princely states created problems viz. Jammu and Kashmir, Junagadh, and Hyderabad. Once the paramountcy lapsed, theoretically they were free to do anything, as terms of accession were not clearly spelt out. ere ruler belonged to one religion, while people majority of them, belonged to another religion. It was assumed that they would join either of the two new states. The will of the people and the will of the ruler were to be taken, its modus operandi again left some gap in clarity.

But Junagadh and Hyderabad had no geographical contiguity to Pakistan, and so were easily by some force were integrated with the Indian Union. Jammu and Kashmir was geographically contagious to both India and Pakistan, and when the tribal irregulars later on baked up by Pakistani army tried to grab Jammu and Kashmir, Pandit Jawaharlal Nehru, the first Prime Minister on India had both the support of the then Dogra ruler Hari Singh and backing of Sheikh Abdullah, leader of National Conference. Once the instrument of Accession was signed by Hari Singh the Hindu ruler, then the government of India sent military force to checkmate the designs of the tribal irregulars and Pakistani army.

The fight was stopped by the United Nations and Cease fire was declared in January 1949, and was endorsed by a resolution of a Security Council. The United Nations supervised the cease fire line and got the agreement of government of India and Pakistan to plebiscite in disputed territory, to be held under the auspices of a United Nations plebiscite Administrator, Admiral Chester Ninitz to the US Navy. But withdrawal of forces into years period did not take place. There was some exchange of communication between Pandit Jawaharlal Nehru and his counterpart Mohammed Ali Bogra, but it just circled around the issue of partition. Since then the stalemated situation has existed till now.

This first Indo-Pak war on Kashmir in the aftermath of partition synchronized with post partition killings which nearly accounted 80,000 lives with barbarity and cruelty searing the psyche and memories, for years to come. Most of the members of the ruling elite in politics, bureaucracy and the army were refugees from India. Also the religious clergy, who wielded lot of authority right from the start in the life of the new nation. So it is not surprising the historical burden of pre-partition time had been a factor to be reckoned with.

Some genealogists of Pakistan do into just remember the Cambridge Student Chaudhari Rehmat Ali in the 1930's but go back to Saladin in twelfth century but even as backwards as the divide between Indus versus Indic cultural regions. This perspective was not shared by ideologues of the Congress Party and many leaders and ordinary people in the country, who believed in oneness of India. Mahatma Gandhi, Maulana Abdul Kalan Azad and others Pandit Nehru, Sardar Patel, C. Rajgopalachari etc accepted the partition plan only when there was the fear of a civil war and the bitter experience of working with the Muslim League in the Interim Government during the time of Viceroyalty of Lord Wavell.

Liaquat Ali Khan the first Prime Minister of Pakistan said in 1950 which was reported in The Hindu, 24th August, 1950 "I charge the government of India first, it has never whole heartedly accepted the partition scheme, but her leaders paid lip service to it merely to get British troops out of the country. Secondly India is out to destroy the state of Pakistan which Indian leaders persistently continue to regard as part of India itself."[1] This strongly held perception is still predominant in Pakistan even now.

The ever arching influence of Muslim League ideology of two-nation theory is so embedded that Liaaquat Ali who was at the helm of affairs from August 1947 – October 1951, when he was mysteriously assassinated revealingly said as reported in The Dawn, 9th October, 1950 that 'I have always considered myself as the

Prime Minister of the League, in every regard myself as the Prime Minister chosen by the members of constituent Assembly'.[2]

This just is contrary to what the Founding Fathers of Indian Constitution envisioned and so the functioning of parliamentary democracy in Independent India is based on different ideology. When Commander-in-chief Ayub Khan became the Martial Law Administrator on October 8, 1958 he said 'my authority is revolution. I have no sanction in law or constitution'. So it is no surprise that Pakistan became garrison state, where three A's were important, Allah, Army and America. The domestic stability and political ideology has much to do with adversial relationship between the two neighbors when Kuldip Nayar called 'Distant Neighbors'. Incidentally it was the title of one of his book. I.K.Gujral the former Prime Minister while delivering V.S. Ram Memorial Lecture at Lukhnow University, November 15, 2002 said " it may be useful to recall that there has never been a war between India and Pakistan when Pakistan was ruled by democratically elected governments". Field Marshal Ayub Khan, General Yahya Khan fell on the wayside because of the 1965 and 1971 second and the third Indo-Pak wars respectively. General turned President Zia Ul Haq and General turned President Pervez Musharraf got a lifeline because of the Afghan wars of 1979 and 2000. in both Afghan wars due to its geo-strategic importance USA made Pakistan its frontline state.

Pakistan is not homogeneous state like Sweden and Japan, and it forges and sustains its identity by the other Hindu nation that is India. Even gender stereotypes are used, that Hindus are like a fickle woman, treacherous and deceitful, and Pakistanis as Muslims are martial race. One Pakistani soldier is equal to four Hindu soldiers. This militates against a better harmonious relationship. Even sports like cricket and hockey are not immune to this. It becomes politicized and is question of pride and national honour.

POST-NUCLEAR PERIOD

The world view shaped by religious ideology, an offshoot

of two nation theory is found even in text books, which lately in our country too is under that pressure. The Nuclear tests which were conducted in Chagai Mountain in state of Baluchistan on May 28, 1998 has story to tell with great historical import. The Directorate of Primary Education in Baluchistan was among the first to incorporate nuclear ideology in school texts. The class V Social Studies textbook produced by the Directorate states " Despite several attempts by Pakistan to establish good relations with India, India did not desist from its dangerous designs. India conducted five nuclear explosions in May 1998 and became an atomic power. Then India began to threaten Pakistan and kept saying that Pakistan would be given the lessons of its life. Upon this provocation, Pakistan conducted five successful nuclear explosions on May 28 and 30, 1998 and managed to shut India up. Now Pakistan is a major atomic power. Its enemies cannot succeed in their designs because Pakistan can now defend itself". And if this is not enough, names of the missiles are Ghazni, Ghauri and Abdali.[3] These invaders from Afghanistan had defeated the Hindu armies during the medieval and modern period.

India has termed its missile as Agni and Prithvi. This has nothing historical in its suggestive or associational dimension. However, history textbooks in India too does not pass muster, when particularly under the present government dispensation of national Democratic Alliance some efforts has been made to tinker with the period of Muslim rule in the land.

The cross of history is there and over its implications Winston Churchill, the war time British Prime Minister had insightfully observed "if we open quarrel between the present and the past, we shall be in danger of losing the future".

Both in domestic politics and foreign policy the direction taken by both the nations were poles apart. Evacuee property compensation claims, division of assets left by the departing British, rehabilitation of refugees, recovery of abducted women etc were tackled in the early post-partition years. Prime Minister Pandit Jawaharlal Nehru and Prime Minister Liaqat Ali Khan met in Delhi in 1950 and resolved to sort out issues connected with communal riots.

Kashmir issue bedeviled relationship between the two neighbors. Pakistan government has a grudge that the last Viceroy Lord Louis Mountbatten played a dubious role in getting the Muslim majority Gurdaspur area divided to give India crucial link with Kashmir through his alleged influence over Sir Cyril Radcliff who had the job of demarcating the boundaries of the two new states. And to boot Radcliff report's publication was well two days after August 15, 1947. That is on August 17, 1947.

PAKISTAN IN SEARCH OF FRIENDS

The post-colonial, post-cold war and post-nuclear period encompasses the fifty-five year period 1947-2002. Pakistan after independence turned its attention towards Muslim nation of West Asia for support and solidarity, but as these nations had their own problems it looked around for a balancer. As it was in conventional military strength not equal to India, its security concerns made it look for allies. The two superpowers in the aftermath of the Second World War found themselves at daggers drawn with each other. Both the United States and Soviet Union had their alliance system, and the cold War had begun.

USA was following the policy of containment of Soviet Union as its putative intellectual father George Kennan had authored an article in prestigious magazine Foreign Affairs under the name X. The communist Revolution spearheaded by Mao-Tse-Tung was victorious over Chiang Ka-Sheikh in 1949. And both the Soviet Union and communist China, followers of communist ideology were looking out for friends amongst the new states of the Third World. The decolonization process had begun in 1947, and British Empire was on retreat. Ofcourse Americans had given freedom to Philippines in 1946.

In this world scenario Pakistan joined the alliance system cobbled up by the United States. It became member of CENTO (Central Treaty Organization) and SEATO (South East Asia Treaty Organization). This was in the decade of 1950's during the Presidency of Dwight Eisenhower. While America provided economic and military aid to Pakistan and so thus helped in modernization of its army and the defense force in general, but the important caveat was that the latter had to help the former against the communist powers in West and East Asia. But Pakistan was not interested in that, but it was more interested in buttressing its military strength vis-à-vis India.

PANDIT NEHRU AND WORLD POLITICS

This riled and antagonized India, and Pandit Nehru had prescience to see that these weapons would be used against India, and the future events vindicated it, the wars of 1965 and of 1971.

The American President Dwight Eisenhower and his Secretary of State John Foster Dulles were not happy with the policy of Non-Alignment[4] which Pandit Jawaharlal Nehru along with other two important leaders Marshal Tito of Yugoslovakia and President Gamal Abdel Nasser had made it influential in world politics. John Foster Dulles was highly critical of its and dubbed it as immoral.

Pandit Nehru strode like a colossus on the international stage and was the one who fashioned the concept of Non-alignment, and the then USSR and communist China used his good office in passing on important message to United States of America. To cite one example is the Korean War in early 1950's. Former President S. Radhakrishnan was India's ambassador to Moscow, and Sardar K. M. Pannikkar was in Beijing during their tenure, raised India's status and image high in comity of nations.

It was India who stood for communist China's representation in United Nations Organizatioon, and at Bandung Conference in 1955, introduced Chou-en-Lai the Prime Minister of the heads of Afro-Asian leaders assembled over there. That was being done by

Pandit Jawaharlal Nehru who was one of the leading lights of the conference, and originator of the idea. It was he who had called Asian Relations Conference in New Delhi in 1947.

"Hindi-Chini Bhai-Bhai" was the buzzword in Indo-Chinese relations and Panchashila agreement was already signed in 1954 when Prime Minister Chou en-Lai had visited New Delhi. It as in late fifties over the boundary issue related to Macmohan Line that gradually led to souring of relations between the two. At Bandung Conference the personal diplomacy of Pakistani Prime Minister Mohammad Ali Bogra strengthened Pakistani and Chinese relationship. He had clarified that Pakistan' participation in South East Asia Treaty Organization no way means that Pakistan would join in any anti communist china military action.

Visit of Nikolai Bulganian and Nikita Khruschev to India in 1955 amidst much hoopla and fanfare cemented Indo-Soviet relationship. Here on Indian soil, Nikita Khruschev had categorically supported India's stand on Kashmir and Goa, and promised economic assistance to boot. Bhilai steel plant in present day Chattisgarh state was the centre piece of the economic aid, and trade was through the exchange of ruble currency. And Soviet veto power was of much help to India in security council debates or resolutions on Kashmir.

Pakistan was tied to the apron-strings of USA and got the bonanza of economic and military aid. Due to the initiative of World Bank president Eugene Black, Indus water treaty was signed on September 19, 1960 when prime Minister Nehru and Hafiz Mohammad Ibrahim the irrigation minister went to Islamabad for the signing ceremony with President Ayub Khan. The crux of the agreement was that India should for irrigation purposes use the easterly streams in the basin Sutlej, Beas and Ravi, while Pakistan would use the three westerly streams Chhenab, Jhelum and Indus. It rounded the decade of 1950's without any serious clashes between the two neighbors.

The triangular relationship between India, Pakistan and communist china underwent radical shifts during the late fifties. Pakistan had given a good chunk of the occupied Kashmir area to communist China, while India faced serious border differences with the latter. This climaxed in Indo-Chinese war in October 1962. The climacteric year when Cuban Missile crisis took place.

Pandit Nehru requested help from both United States and United Kingdom. Despite Nehru's reservation, President Dwight Eisenhower did not stop aiding Pakistan, likewise despite Pakistan's amazement and aversion President John F. Kennedy responded to plea of non-aligned India. John Kenneth Galbraith was US ambassador to India and was friend of both President Kennedy and Pandit Nehru. President Kennedy infact also wrote to President Ayub Khan to the effect that the latter would not open any military front against beleaguered India. United Kingdom too responded positively.

Soviet Union was no way going to help communist China in this border conflict with India with whom it also had good relationship. Averrel Harriman roving ambassador of USA and Duncan Sandys, British Foreign Secretary were sent by their respective governments to help in resolution of the Kashmir problem. But after a series of meetings between foreign ministers of both the countries Sardar Swaran Singh and Zulfikar Ali Bhutto stretching over six months period alternating in Pakistani and Indian cities, the mediatory exercise reached a dead-end. Pakistan wanted diplomatic pressure exerted by western powers, which was not forthcoming. Nehru also received assurances from Harriman and Sandys that continual military aid to India was not conditional on settlement of the Kashmir issue. The Chinese made unilateral ceasefire, and the bitter episode so far India was concerned, left Pakistan high and dry.

Pakistan as it remained a revisionist power rather a status quoist, had viewed Kashmir 'as unfinished agenda of the partition' and went first for a skirmish on Rann of Kutch and then launched a full blown conflict in 1965. Rann of Kutch issue was eventually settled through the medium of arbitration by the International Court of Justice. However the war of September-October 1965 was again a stalemated one, and Soviet Union brokered the peace at Tashkent, February 1966. The Prime Minister Alexie Kosygin and Foreign Minister Andrie Gromoka spent full nine days in sorting out the differences between the two heads of State, President Ayub Khan and Prime Minister Lal Bahadur Shastri. One aside is called for.

Prime Minister Jawaharlal Nehru died on May 27, 1964, and it was thought that the Indian Prime Minister Shastri would not be man of steel, so the opportunity for military means was resorted to. Plus the ripple effect of Indo-Chinese war of 1962. The matter was squarely put by Prime Minister Shastri when he told his counterpart "Mr. President, it will annoy you of course to hear this, but we cannot give up Kashmir". Same thing with vehemence was spoken by Andrie Gromyoko to belligerent Zulfikar Ali Bhutto the Foreign Minister that as Pakistan has not won the war, Soviet Union cannot offer you Kashmir. There was controversy over the wording of the draft in which peaceful resolution of the problem would be chosen instrumentality. Not the words without resort to force.

The situation was restored as it was before the war, and respective combatants returned the territory which they conquered of the other. The Indian Foreign Secretary C.S. Jha's draft which he had taken to the conference at Tashkent was accepted by and large by the Soviet interlocutors.

It needs mentioning that President Lyndon. B. Johnson had sent his advisor and veteran diplomat to Peshawar with a personal message which he handed it over at the Peshawar to President Ayub Khan who was on his way to Tashkent airport for attending the conference. This meant US approval of Soviet effort to broker peace, and in which US also wanted to remain in the picture.

Post-Tashkent phase of Indo-Pakistani relationship witnessed domestic upheavals till 1992. Split in the Congress party in India in 1969, and the opposition turning their fusillade on her for being soft on Pakistan. The war of 1971 and the emergence of an independent state of Bangladesh, Sikh insurgency, Zulfiquar Ali Bhutto's rise to power and his fall ending in his death by hanging in 1977. The Soviet invasion of Afghanistanin 1979, this synchronized with the fall of Shah of Iran the same year. The assassination of Mujibur Rehman, Indira Gandhi and Rajiv Gandhi, occurred in the period 1965-1992 which also saw the removal of two Pakistani heads of state – Field Marshall Ayub Khan and General Yahya Khan. And the mysterious death in air crash of another head of state General Zia -ul -Haq in 1986.

The domestic upheaval in Pakistan's eastern wing was sparked by trial of Sheikh Mujibur Khan and others known as Agartala conspiracy of 1968 led to General Yahya Khan's ordering of General Tikka Khan to suppress the uprising. Sheikh Mujibur Rehman had been in touch with Indian diplomatic and intelligence community people. The influx of refugees into West Bengal left India no option and it led to 1971 war. President Richard M. Nixon displayed his tilt and ordered the American ship Enterprise in Bay of Bengal. However, Indian military victory, created apprehensions in minds of American administration and George Bush senior who was US representative in UN asked pointed questions to Indians in the Security Council "Does India intend to destroy the Pakistan Army in the West...to annex territory in West Pakistan?, to take parts of Pakistan-controlled Kashmir contrary to the Security council resolutions of 1948, 49 and 50? The world has a right to know what India's intentions are." Sardar Swaran Singh, the Foreign Minister at noon on December 18, 1971 declared before the Security Council that neither West Pakistan or of Bangladesh by conquest or otherwise, India wants to acquire. Jack Anderson's investigative reporting revealed that USA during the war helped Pakistan through Saudi Arabia.

SIMLA AGREEMENT, 1971

Despite India's victory Prime Minister Indira Gandhi concluded the Simla Agreement with her counterpart Zulfiquar Ali Bhutto without full utilization of diplomatic trumps in her hands. Bangladesh emerged as an independent nation. And it was agreed that Indo-Pakistan differences would be resolved bilaterally and the Kashmir question would not be raised in international forums.

Zulfiquar Ali Bhutto the Pakistani head of the State gave a new direction to the foreign policy of Pakistan. There was marked disenchantment with USA. He had not forgotten that when he went as Foreign Minister to attend John F. Kennedy's funeral in Washington the new President Lyndon B. Johnson had shown his displeasure with his flirtation with China and President Soekarno of Indonesia.

Field Marshall Ayub Khan's book *'Friends Not Masters'* and Zulfiquar Ali Bhutto's own book *'The Myth of Independence'*: the very titles are very revealing. In his interview with David Frost, President Nixon when he was not more in office said that despite Treaty of Friendship which Mrs. Indira Gandhi had signed prior to military action, he was not going to allow Soviet Union to allow India to gobble up West Pakistan. And he wanted China also to not of his intention, though China did not intervene which was fondly hoped by General Yahya Khan, it backed up Pakistan. It declared that it would withhold recognization to Bangladesh till India released all 91,000 Pakistani prisoners of war.

Zulfiquar Ali Bhutto as Prime Minister in post 1971 period till his fall from power by coup maker Zia-ul-Haq in July 1977, turned the parameters of Pakistan's foreign policy. He hosted Islamic conference in Lahore 1972. He was pro-Arab in Arab-Israel dispute. He associated his country with non-aligned nations and the group of 77 at United Nations Organizations, and after 1973 got lot of funds from Saudi Arabia, Kuwait and other oil rich sheikhdoms not excluding Gaddafi of Libya for making of an Islamic bomb.

Lot of Pakistani workers also went to West Asia for jobs, and their remittances helped the Pakistani economy. He withdrew Pakistan from the Commonwealth in 1972. He was very pro-Chinese, and also endeavored to mend fences with Soviet Union. General Zia-ul-Haq who toppled him from power in 1977 gave much impetus to Islamisation of Pakistani society. His policy of Nizam-i-Mustafa and Nizam-i-islam made him popular with clergy and orthodox elements of society. He joined Non-Aligned Movement in 1979, when President Fidel Castro of Cuba invited Pakistan to the Havana Summit held over there.

India had opposed Pakistan's admission into the Non-Aligned conferences so far, and it opposed the re-admission of Pakistan into the Commonwealth. Pakistan had opposed India's participation in Islamic Conference meting at Rabat, Morocoo in 1969. So at various forum like at United Nations Organization or at SAARC (South Asian Association for Regional Cooperation) both have clashed for posts or clashed because of different policies and perspectives.

Post-Simla Accord, July 2, 1972 which came in the wake of Third Indo-Pakistani war till 2002, there were near hits and misses except for the costliest Kargil misadventure launched by Pakistan during the Prime Ministership of Nawaz Sharif. The military exercises along the border in 1987 (Operation Brasstacks) and of 1990 was very near run. The Foreign Ministers meetings and the coming of President Zia-ul-Haq to watch cricket match at Jaipur defused the tension. In 1990 Robert Gates mission to India helped the situation from going out of control.

Seymour Hersh[5] thought events of 1990 were quite serious and he wrote an article '*On the Nuclear Edge*' in the issue of March 20, 1993 for the '*New Yorker*' magazine. Recently in issue of December 23, 2002 the Indian magazine '*India Today*'[6] it carried an article that on January 24 and June 10,2002 India came very close to war with Pakistan. Few issues like Siachen Glacier, The

Sir Creek and The Tulbul Wular dispute is still hanging fire, but it gets sidelined in the glare and heat of Kashmir tangle.

NUCLEARISATION OF THE CONFLICT

Pokharan I explosion on May 18, 1974 inaugurated a new phase in relationship with nuclear dimension. From this date to May 11,1998, Pakistan was in search for an Islamic bomb. And on May 28, 1998 it conducted its nuclear tests. India since the first Pokharan test in 1974 adopted the policy of nuclear abstinence though had been critical of the nuclear apartheid regime, an exclusive club of white nations with China as a non-white entrant.

US administration through Symington, Pressler, Glenn amendment had tried to stop the nuclear ambition of Pakistan, but it was a unavailing. President Jimmy Carter made the French government from anyway helping Pakistan in its goal, and it backed out. However, the father of Pakistani nuclear bomb, though others are also staking their claim, Dr. Khan had been successful in purloining the designs etc from Holland. Communist China was too in the picture.

India after the first Pokharan test in 1974 found USA stopping the fuel for Tarapure reactor. And after both the nations doing multiple tests in May 1998, sanctions and withholding of aid was the end result.

The US administration had been long working for Nuclear Non-Proliferation and since 1960's had been trying to get nations sign Nuclear Non-Proliferation Treaty (NPT), Comprehensive Test Ban Treaty, Fissile Material Cut-off Agreement. But it has not been very successful. Iraq and North Korea for example who had signed Nuclear Non-Proliferation Treaty are in the docks.

India feels concerned of her security due to close friendship between Pakistan and China. Representative Sherred Brown (Democrat-Ohio) writing in *India Abroad*, July31 ,1998 said that China had sold M-II missiles to Pakistan, may even have put nuclear weapons in Tribet, and has completed de facto encirclement of India . Vladmikr Putin had said recently there is fear that Pakistani nukes may fall into the hands of militants or *Jehadi* groups. President Pervez Musharraf's recent statement of even using nuclear weapon, in case Indian troops cross Line of Control (LOC) elicited an editorial comment[7] in the *Asian Age* of January 2, 2003. It says 'Unencumbered by any sense of responsibility. General Pervez Musharraf signed off the year gone by on characteristically cavalier notes: by indulging in nuclear blackmail.' Saudi Arabia has been financing Islamabad's nuclear and missile purchases from China.

In this dismissal scenario confidence security building Measures which had come vague since the Helsinki accord of 1975 has provided lifeline to both the conflictual neighbors to save themselves from any miscalculation of intension, accidents etc. The director general of Military Operation of both the countries communicates with each other every week. The hot line, advance notice of military exercises, eschewal of chemical weapons is various resources in the nuclear stability assistance program. Both have agreed not to attack each others nuclear installations, and very recently they have once again reaffirmed their earlier agreement, which is a good omen.

The Pakistani ship Ghazi was sunk off the coast of Karachi in 1971 war, and since then Pakistan has developed its naval strength and wants its presence felt as far as its influence can go. Though Indian navy has built up its naval muscle its influence in Indian Ocean and Arabian Sea has grown, and US as a sole Superpower now has joint naval exercises etc., with the former.

There is one significant development since 1971 war, that conventional military wars have been relegated to the background. Soldiers in military uniforms fighting over well-marked territorial area has given way to covert army units, paramilitary formation, mushrooming terrorist organization, insurgents, mercenaries encompassing many nationalities, shadowy intelligence agencies who have made mincemeat of territorial boundaries. Abetted and financed by neighboring countries, well backed with multiple resources by diasporic communities girdling the globe, they are wreaking havoc against the enemy's soft targets, installations and infrastructure.

HIJACKING : ANOTHER DIMENSION OF THE CONFLICT

On July 6,1984 Indian Airlines Air Bus was hijacked by Sikh terrorists to Lahore. Plane, passengers, crew were returned but not the hijackers. In December 1999, an Indian Airlines from Kathamandu was hijacked allegedly by Pakistani militants, and held captive for a week in Kandar in Afghanisstan. One passenger was killed, and India had to release a hardcore leader of terrorist organization imprisoned in New Delhi jail. And for which the Indian Foreign minister Jaswant Singh had to go along with him in plane Kandhar.

Low intensity conflict since 1989 in Kashmir aided and abetted by Pakistan has given new lease of life to cross-border terrorism. If Pakistan had backed up Sikh insurgency, trained Naga militants on its soil at behest of the Chinese, planting ISI operatives in Bangladesh and within India, likewise India had not been averse to give boost to Pakhtunistan movement or to help Mujubhir Rahman and other dissidents of former East Pakistan . Mohajir leader Altaf based in London likes to cultivate New Delhi and it is reciprocated. This support to each other's dissident groups has not added much to amity, but has caused bitterness. Giving funds and wherewithal and sanctuary are some of the ways to annoy the other side. Pakistan on and off indulges in manhandling and abduction of Indian diplomatic personnel in its territory.

AFGHANISTAN: FACTOR IN INDO-PAK RELATIONS

Since the end of Cold War and the break-up of former Soviet Union, its influence and clout in the sub-continent has diminished The Soviet Union invasion of Afghnistan in 1979, had given USA an opportunity to make it their Vietnam. Pakistan became the frontline state, and it became just about the fourth nation in the world to get American economic and military aid.

For India, Communist China and Afghanistan had posed many problems. Both have put New Delhi in the back foot. Osama-bin-Laden and Al-Qaeda group with their supporter Mullah Omar and the Taliban changed the world scenario when the former on September 11,2001 masterminded the attack on World Trade Centre, New York and Pentagon in Washington D.C.

This brought USA again in another way to Afhganistan to root out Osama-bin-Laden and his Al-Qaeda group and its patron Taliban government. In the bargain General Parvez Musharraf had no choice but to become the frontline state for USA. And in words of former Foreign Minister Jaswant Singh, the epicenter of terrorism now found home in Pakistan.

In the balance-sheet one finds the conflictual relationship between two proximate neighbors sharing nearly 6000 kilometer boundary lay in its history – before and after partition. The religious ideology of two-nation theory had made it very acrimonious. Pandit Jawaharlal Nehru to Atal Bihari Vajpayee always wanted to keep outside powers away from the sub-continent. Whether it was non-alignment or Gujral doctrine it had the same goal of settling dispute through bilateral means. However, both the power brought outside powers into the arena of Indo-Pakistan dispute right on the centre stage of history.

SAARC (South Asian Association for Regional Cooperation) became the arena also of bilateral acrimony of both India and Pakistan. Its dream of becoming like ASEAN or ECC is just a chimera. Pakistan has not given Most Favored Nations status to India, and it prefers to buy items though costly like Tea or Iron Ore from other nations. It is no surprising both lose revenue, when there is flourishing illegal trade. Gas reserves from Iran or Central Asian Republic, which means laying down pipe through Pakistan, may see victory of geo-strategy rather geo-economy.

The Lahore Declaration of Prime Minister Nawaj Sharif and Prime Minister Atal Bihari Vajpayee in February, 1999 and Agra Summit between General Pervez Musharraf and Atal Bihari Vajpayee in July 2001 yielded no positive result.

CONCLUDING COMMENTS

India is having fourth largest Army in the World while Pakistan is having the eighth largest Army in the World. And both are buying Weapons from all possible sources. India is no more averse in buying from Israel.

The cost of weaponisation on civil society is very high. Not only the money, but the causalities are ordinary citizens-men, women and children. Old and young, poor and rich, and the bullet know or respect no religion of the victim.

The diasporic community in their vicarious and empty pleasure of nostalgia pumps money and weapons, if possible. Mehaboob-ul-Haq in his report on Human Development in South Asia in 1997 states "If India and Pakistan can reduce their defense expenditure, they can finance their entire social agenda in the next 15 years and can fulfill all of the (social) services with additional $8 billion coming from peace dividends". Amartya Sen, the Nobel prize winner economists too things on similar lines.

Various American Foundation like Rand, Hudson, Heritage, Salzburg seminar, Neemrana Fort deliberation, candle light ceremony at Waugh border etc. and Track 2 diplomacy have strengthened in whatever small way in building bridges of understanding. Books, magazines, seminars, news papers non-governmental organizations, human rights bodies etc. have fleshed out many confidence-building security measures. Think Tanks and Defense Analysis institutes too have put in their mite.

Maleeha Lodhi, one time Ambassador of Pakistan to USA has rightly said that peace making can be reinforced by Track II or citizens diplomacy in which NGO's could play a role. Many men and women of good will of both the countries are needed to build bonds of amity amongst the people.

France-Germany, Britain-France hostility of long standing centuries have been buried and perhaps it is a question of long haul. We have only 55 years of freedom. Today USA and CANADA share a long unguarded border, and both the nation enjoys perfect harmony except for some momentary hiccups.

India and Pakistan cannot afford to live on just passing the buck for everything wrong in their relationship. That is blaming the British for everything from 'divide and rule' policy to neo-colonialism. Of course they have done grave mistake, but now both have to work it out .

The Indo-Pakistani relationship is also a love and hate relationship. Many Indian Muslims have their relative of other side and the same is true on the reverse side.

Many people from north India have nostalgic memories of Lahore and other cities now in Pakistan.

Today the supreme is to contain violence and mayhem which is deterritorialized. And a new paradigm is needed where security is not state-oriented but people-oriented.

India has to make its secular foundation more strong and solid while Pakistan has to think how can it make its state modern squaring up to the principles of Islam, and how to enjoy the positive fruits of modernity without losing their religion. One track obsession over Kashmir would mean deferment of better future.

REFERENCES :

1. *The Hindu,* 24 August 1950.
2. *The Dawn,* 9 October 1950.
3. Mahmud Ghazani invaded India 17 times during early 11 century. Mohammad Ghauri who killed Prithviraj Chauhan in the second battle of Tarain 1192 A.D.

Ahmad Shah Abdali defeated forces of Maratha Confederacy under the leadership of Sadashiv Bhau in the Third Battle of Panipat, 1761. All these were Afghan invaders who defeated the Hindu armies .

Pakistani Missiles are named after these invaders, which reveals their embedded hatred.

4. Non-Alignment is a policy fashioned by Pandit Jawaharlal Nehru (India) , Gamal Abdel Nasser (Egypt) and Marshal Tito (Yugoslovakia) as a response to Cold War generated in the world soon after the World War II due to two Superpowers USA and USSR rivalry. Its main thrust was not to get embroiled In Superpower rivalry and to keep itself away from joining any alliance bloc.

5. Seymour Hersh, "On the Nuclear Edge": *New Yorker*, 20 March 1993.

6. Shushir Gupta , "When India Came Close to War", *India Today*, 13 December 2002,p.25.

7. Editorial, *The Asian Age* ,2 January 2003.

3

INDO-PAK RELATIONS Geo-Political and Strategic Dimensions

Vijay Kumar

If foes commit an outrage on
A house, and one forgives —
Be it from fear or greed — he is
The meanest man that lives

—The Panchtantra[1]

India and Pakistan have maintained at best a conflictual and tumultuous relationship. Their relations have never been smooth since their vivisection on the eve of Independence in 1947. Even during the periods of relative peace and calm, there has always been a perceptual aggressive mood ready to burst even with veiled/pseudo provocation of forces— either internal or external. The recent nuclearization of both powers has not only intensified their conflict, but has actually pushed South Asia in a critical nuclear zone threshold threatening South Asian security in particular and world peace in general. The world's political geography, international economic relations, regional and global power structures, the strategic perceptions, shifting focus of security and the aims and methods of warfare have undergone tremendous changes in recent years, which has considerable impact on Indo-Pak geo-political and strategic concerns. These two actors have been very conscious to the emerging challenges and opportunities thrown up by the changing international environment and are still staggering under pre- and post-partition hangover.

THE FOCUS

Carved out of a "**successful foreign policy**" pursued in pre-independence period by the leadership of the Muslim League, [2] Pakistan was beset with a myriad of problems since its inception. It was a divided, incomplete and partial homeland for the Muslims. The legacy of the partition and the dispute with India burdened the psyche of Pakistan to search for its security in an environ of conflictual and adversial relationship in the South-Asian sub-system. The creation of Bangladesh and the surrender of nearly a lakh of well-equipped Pakistani soldiers continued to haunt and remained firmly rooted in the mind of Pakistani leadership. Periodic wars, border strives, rivalries and occasional Kargil type standoffs kept on adding salt to the injury of tumultuous relationship.

The continuing tension in over 50 years of their independent existence — their overt and convert love-hate relationship, have been rooted in traditional tangible issues and stereotyped mindsets, fixed images and faulty perceptions besides successive failure of democracy to take roots in Pakistan. These factors assume an added intensification in the wake of persistent efforts by different domestic and foreign elements to furl over their narrow political interests.

The aim of this paper is to discuss the geo-political and strategic dimensions of Indo-Pak relationship in historical perspective and bring out the futility, the hollowness of their bickering at a time when the world is going global razing national identities to the ground.

UNENDING CONFLICT AND ANIMOSITY

In the post-war period, two regional conflicts have grown parallel to the Cold-War itself. These two are Indo-Pakistan rivalry in South Asia and Arab-Israel conflict in West Asia.[3] Though the Cold-war has ceased to exist with the dismemberment of Soviet Union, these two have defied all peace processes. Fifty-odd years of separation and independent existence of India and Pakistan have not been enough to stunt the seeds of discord, mutual distrust and suspicion. Even today their relations are bedeviled by a host of contentious issues having their origin in the pre-partition days. Three major military conflicts, Kargil episode and India's military deployment on the borders after December 13, 2001, terrorist attack on Indian Parliament have kept the cup of their embittered relations overflowing.

Indo-Pak relations stand on a different footing from what normally such relations should be between two neighbouring states because of the particular circumstances in which Pakistan came into existence, consequently, hostility towards India has been the mainstay of successive governments of Pakistan. Undeniably, therefore, the basic underlying motive of Pakistan's foreign policy has been rivalry with India. Being the part of the same larger group at one time, Pakistan's innate ambition is to gain as much influence, prestige and strength as India and to make as much progress as India is making. Pakistan, in other words, seeks to establish parity equation with India through confrontation and conflict rather than rapprochement, co-operation and peace.[4] In their conflict and rivalry they have kept their eyes closed to the changes that have swept the world demolishing barriers between nations and people. They have failed to take lessons from the fall of the Berlin Wall in 1989 which symbolize the end of Cold War, and have released sweeping waves of globalization and liberalization knitting together the world as a unit.

PAKISTAN PERCEPTION : SEARCH FOR SECURITY AGAINST INDIA

Geo-political factors have been the warp and waft of this rivalry which had its impact on conflict and aggressive postures of Pakistan against India. In Pakistan's thinking and security perception economic development, preservation and promotion of Islamic ideals have been the strongest foreign policy interests from the very beginning. Pakistan's first Prime Minister, Liaquat Ali Khan had three major interests in mind [5]

(i) Integrity of Pakistan ;

(ii) Promotion of Pakistan's culture, i.e., the Islamic way of life; and

(iii) Economic development.

Field Marshal Ayub Khan talked about mainly "security and development" as objectives of his foreign policy. Security for him included not only "the defence of our country" but also the "preservation of our ideology" which meant by implication the preservation of Islamic culture.[6] Despite a major shift in the foreign policy of Pakistan under Zulfiquar Bhutto, there persisted a marked continuity in so far as the primary objective of preserving the integrity and security of the country was concerned. "The inevitable first object of foreign policy", wrote Keith Callard, "had to be to show the world that Pakistan was a reality and was capable of maintaining its independence."[7] Bhutto had "matured in an atmosphere of passionate and fanatical zeal among the Muslims to prove the viability, necessity and inevitability of Pakistan,"[8] as such his policy of "bilateralism" brought him close to the Muslim world and especially the Persian Gulf states. Strengthening of fraternal relations among Muslim countries based on "Islamic Unity and Brotherhood" was also mentioned in the Constitution of 1973. The same policy of search for security against India and other immediate neighbours, economic development, preservation and promotion of Islamic culture have remained the running thread of Pakistan's foreign policy under successive regimes of either brand — civil or military. As Pakistan was disenchanted with USA, Bhutto leaned toward Pan-Islamism.

SENSE OF INSECURITY

The 'insecurity syndrome' in Pakistan's policy has been prominent from the very beginning. Ayub Khan said :

We have our security problem with India since partition. India's foreign policy and its policy towards Pakistan has been offensive and non-cooperative.[9]

A political analyst has put the facts succintly in the following words :

The quest for security has been the dominating factor in the foreign policy objectives. In search for security against a potential Indian threat, Pakistan turned to the Commonwealth and to the Muslim countries in the early years of the independence (1947-53); then she turned to the USA by entering into a number of bilateral and multilateral defensive pacts. Then in the 1960's Pakistan found that the Western allies had upset the balance of power in the subcontinent by arming India against China, arms which Pakistanis felt could well be used against them; the Russians also joined in helping the Indians in their huge military build-up after the Sino-Indian border conflict of 1962. Pakistan, therefore, turned to new friends, if not allies, in the same search for security.[10]

Bhutto's and subsequent regime's policies too were guided by the same sense of insecurity vis-a-vis India. In one of his speeches as Foreign Minister in National Assembly in March 1966 Bhutto expressed his fears of India thus :

India cannot tolerate the existence of Pakistan .... India on the pretext of the struggle of the people of Kashmir wanted to destroy Pakistan .... because in the destruction of Pakistan lay India's most sublime and finest dreams.[11]

Pakistan's military defeat at the hands of India in December 1971 war, foundation of the People's Republic of Bangladesh as an independent state from the territory of East Pakistan, and the drastic change in power relations in South Asian sub-continent forced the Pakistanis to reconsider its relation with India for the time being. But Simla accord was projected by their leaders as a "triumph" for Pakistan, Bhutto "emerged with Pakistan's territory intact" and convinced the people of Pakistan that "Simla was not a sell-out".[12] Ashok Kapur has shown that Pakistan's defeat in Bangladesh war became a dominant affair in "Pakistan nuclear and arms control affairs. For the first time in Pakistan's nuclear history, and its domestic politics, the nuclear programme was given an explicit anti-India and military focus."[13]

NUCLEAR PARITY WITH INDIA

Bhutto's dreams of attaining parity with India in nuclear field have fructified. His famous statement of eating grass for a thousand years but getting a Islamic bomb became a reality in May 1998 when in response to India's five detonations of nuclear devices, Pakistan answered by exploding six. General Pervez Musharraf on January 4, 2000 stated that Pakistan would not hesitate to use nuclear weapons if its security was threatened. In his words "If the security of Pakistan is threatened, surely we would not allow Pakistan to die. That will not be allowed." He said this in an interview with CNN while replying to a question under what condition would Pakistan be prepared to use nuclear weapons. The Chief Executive admitted that no modalities and principles have yet been prepared but "surely Pakistan's security will never be compromised."[14]

After December 13, 2001 attack by terrorists on Indian Parliament, things reached a flashpoint. India deployed its forces along the borders with Pakistan. Pakistan too responded immediately. Reports from Pakistan indicated that by early January missiles directed against India were put in place. M-11 and M-9 missiles with strike range varying from 600 to 750 Km, Ghauri-I and II with a range of 1150 to 1500 Km and Shaheen II with a range of 2500 Kms were ready for action. India's missile system too was placed in strategic position. The Indian Defence Minister George Fernandes said "At the moment we are concentrating on Agni-II missile with a range of 2500 Km. We do not have any plans now for a longer range missile."[16] On January 24, 2000, while inaugurating an international conference on Asian Security in New Delhi, Defence Minister had declared "India's readiness to fight any limited conventional war under the nuclear shadow."[17] Prime Minister Atal Behari Vajpayee too was forthright. He is quoted to have said :

If Pakistan thinks we are going to wait for it to launch the first bomb, it is wrong. If Pakistan wants to avoid a nuclear holocaust, it should accept our proposal for a mutual pact against nuclear aggression."[18]

INDIA : A WHIPPING BOY FOR PAKISTAN

It would thus not be an exaggeration to point out that India has been a factor that has primarily determined the foreign policy imperatives of Pakistan. One can hardly refute that Pakistan has found India a "convenient whipping boy in order to foster unity within its own border and curb any unrest of differences among its own people."[19] Whenever there have been internal problems they have been put down by raising the Indian bogey.This psychotic fear of Pakistan has been due to many mutual problems.

In Pakistan's thinking and action, security against Indian designs have been given priority because of the following major factors :

- *the opposition of Indian leaders to the creation of Pakistan until the last moment of their agreement to it.*
- *dream of united India even after partition by certain sections of the Indian society.*
- *India's continued denunciation of the two-nation theory to which Pakistan owes its existence.*
- *the long and bitter relations between the two national forces*

— the Muslim League and the Indian National Congress — which took over power in Pakistan and India respectively.

- *the communal holocaust and violence at the time of partition which left a million dead and ten million uprooted, helped animosities on both sides simmering.*
- *differences over partition of assets and liabilities of undivided India.*
- *dispute over the accession of native states like Junagarh, Hyderabad and Jammu & Kashmir.*
- *India received two-thirds of the military stores and equipments of British India and retained all ordnance factories.*
- *Pakistan in comparison to India was a small country with little economic resources. It had neither adequate stock of coal or steel nor the amount of public or private capital that India commanded.*
- *the two wings of Pakistan, East and West, were separated from each other by 1,100 miles of Indian territory.*
- *East Pakistan was surrounded on three sides by Indian territory and the only approach to it for the West Pakistan was through sea.*
- *security of Pakistan was complicated by Indian control over Jammu and Kashmir. Indian forces could easily outflank the main defended positions of Punjab.*
- *while Pakistan inherited the fields and lower irrigation facilities of the Indus Valley — that part of the Indian sub-continent which is extremely arid and would be desert but for the fact that it is the largest irrigated plain in the world — the headwaters of the Indus Valley were under the control of India. India could devastate the agriculture of West Pakistan by simply controlling the waters of these two rivers.*
- *more than anything else, Pakistan feels that it is incomplete without Jammu and Kashmir. Indian retention of Kashmir,*

> *a predominantly Muslim populated state, refutes the whole validity of the two-nation theory on which Pakistan is based.*[20] *Naturally, the Kashmir question has remained a vital bone of contention from the beginning of its existence.*

In view of the above, Pakistan has always felt that it was handicapped from the very beginning of its existence because of the political manoeuvre of the Indian leaders and its people. Pakistan began its existence as a divided, incomplete and partial homeland for the Indian Muslims. Pakistan was born, in the words of its first leader, Mohammad Ali Jinnah as a "moth-eaten, truncated" version of the original design[21]. because of the political machinations of Indian leaders. India, therefore, remains the enemy number one.. Indian hand in the creation of an independent Bangladesh has further heightened this feeling of animosity.

PRESENT SCENARIO : THE LOOMING NUCLEAR THREAT

History proves that Indo-Pak decision making is heavily influenced by past experience of the two-nations dating back to mainly pre-independence time. The ideological differences between the majority communities of Pakistan and India have been exploited by fundamentalist elements in both the countries to create malice and hatred which has etched stereotyped images to be exploited at will by the political leaders.[22] In the present environment of tension on the borders, lack of proper communication, hostile propaganda and threatening statement, stereotyped images and predispositions still affect decision-making process both in India and Pakistan. Seen in the backdrop of massive Indian capabilities in human, material and technological fields, the hostility of Pakistan keeps growing. Indian success in nuclear missile and space fields, added with its conventional warfare capabilities to meet any future challenges, poses a great threat to Pakistan. India's history of military collaborations with countries like US, Russia, France, Israel too is seen with fear. It is true that the Indian nuclear strategic compass covers “lots more besides Pakistan” because India has to take into account the Persian Gulf region, West Asia, Asia-Pacific and Indian Ocean if it wants to retain its regional power status.[23]

Pakistan has read political designs against itself from India’ first nuclear explosion in 1974 to its five explosions in 1998. No doubt, they have added unprecedented qualitative superiority in India’s balance leaving Pakistan in a state of strategic predicament. But then in terms of capabilities India is the fifth largest country of the world, second in population, fourth in armed forces, tenth in industrial potential (including defence industry), third largest pool of technical and scientific manpower, sixth nuclear power and fourth to launch its own satellite.[24] Its offensive missile capabilities and its blue-water navy are equipped to project its power beyond the region.

Compared to this Pakistan is strategically handicapped against Indian military might. India has 3 : 1 superiority ratio in army, 5:1 in air force and 7 : 1 in navy besides enormous resources in men and material.[25] (See Appendix for a comparative figure on combat strength).

A WORD OF CAUTION

However, history provides the evidence that nuclear weapons solve no purpose and can best be treated as deterrents. So far these have not been used in any of the wars fought by the two nuclear powers However ,the twilight zone of nuclear blackmail remain in the background. The Kargil episode shows that though both India and Pakistan possessed nuclear missiles they did not use these and used only conventional weapons. But low-intensity warfare on the borders and along Line of Control are a cause of concern not only for the two countries but for the whole world because there are chances of miscalculations and accidents which can lead to nuclear catastrophe. In such a situaion friendly overtures, continuous dialogues, people to people contacts should be developed and widened and measures should be taken by both governments to reduce hostilities and end past animosities.

FRIGHTENING DEVELOPMENT REALITIES

The South Asian region, particularly Indo-Pak, has attracted unprecedented international attention in recent times. America's war against "terror" triggered off by September 11, 2001 tragic event and the military action in Afghanistan has seen Pakistan emerge as its reliable ally. The whole of the Western World is looking at India to unlock its enormous economic potential for them. China's active military presence in Tibet and Sinkiang and its active co-operation with Pakistan has both bilateral as well as regional implications. SAARC has been badly affected by historical animosities , religious and socio-political differences of these two nations which have blocked regional co-operation to the degree expected. The regional arms race, involving not only conventional weapons but nuclear arms as well, imposes severe costs for these two poor societies and pose obstacles to economic growth and social justice. In Pakistan, the alarming disparity between the rich and the poor is mind boggling. 66 per cent of all industrial projects, 97 per cent of all insurance funds and 80 per cent of all bank deposits are in the hands of some 20 powerful feudal families.

The Human Development Report, Asia, 1999published under the aegis of UNO, pointed out that the defence spending of Pakistan and India have increased by 14 and 8.5 per cent respectively. The report revealed that this extra expenditure has not only resulted in elimination of the region's poverty but has also given rise to extreme income inequalities. The richest one-fifth of South Asia's population earns almost 40 per cent of the region's income and the poorest one-fifth earns less than 10 per cent. This region is home to more than 560 million poor people of which 300 million people have little to eat. There are 380 million people who are illiterate and 200 million people who have no access to safe drinking water. It is home to 800 million people who have no access even to basic sanitation facilities.[26]

The post-Cold War order has drawn our attention to the interplay between international, regional and national peace, security and development. Poverty, food insecurity, competition over scarce resources, environmental degradation, migration of people, drugs and arms, terrorism, ethnic and religious conflicts now pose more serious threats to regional and national peace. The political behaviour of decision makers in both India and Pakistan seem to be determined by the old vested interests. But the emerging demands for social security cannot be overlooked for long. The question of human security has gained precedence and cannot be relegated to the background for long. The Indo-Pak confrontations have bled both the countries and are a constant drain on their economic and moral resources which otherwise could have been used for the welfare of the teeming millions. The conflicts have also proved a strain on India's secular character.

SUMMING UP

At a time when the concept of security is changing from "security is not just territory" to "security of people through development" without use of arms, there is an urgent need for both these countries to rethink their relationship. Both countries have continued to mess up their relations since 1947, raising monuments to hollow diplomacy, showing a passion for hair-splitting , which never ceases to amaze outsiders. They have poured money into an arms race which mocks their poverty. Their wars have settled nothing and opened no path of peace as wars, paradoxically, often do.[27] A time now has come for both the nations to embrace Development Diplomacy putting in this process, their arms aside and sorting out their problems for peace and prosperity in the region and the world.

REFERENCES :

1. The Story of Unforgiving Monkey, Arthur W. Ryder (Tr.) in Lin Yutang (ed.),*The Wisdom of India*, London : Michael Joseph, 1948 ed., p.15

2. Wayne Wilcox "Pakistan" in Wayne Wilcox, Leo E. Rose and Gavin Boyd (eds.), *Asia and the International System*, Cambridge, Mass : Winthrop, 1972, p.93.
3. See for details, Moonis Ahmad, "Indo-Pak Conflict Resolution : Lessons from the Arab-Israeli Peace Process", *Bangladesh Institute of International and Strategic Studies Journal*, Dacca, Vol.17 (2).
4. Keith B.Callard, *Pakistan, A Political Study*, New York : Macmillan, 1957, Chapter one.
5. Liaquat Ali Khan,*Pakistan, The Heart of Asia*, Cambridge, Mass : Harvard University Press, 1950, pp. 11-12.
6. Mohammad Ayub Khan, *Friends Not Masters : A Political Autobiography,* London : Oxford University Press, 1967, p.114.
7. Callard, *Op.Cit*., p.303.
8. Piloo Mody, *Zulfi, My Friend*, Delhi : Thompson, 1973, p.68.
9 Mohammad Ayub Khan, *Speeches and Statements*, Vol.4; Karachi : Pakistan Publications, N.D., p.83.
10. G.W. Choudhury, Cited in Norman D. Palmer, "Pakistan : The Long Search for Foreign Policy" in Lawrence Ziring, Ralph Braibanti and W.Howard Wriggins (eds.) *Pakistan : The Long View*, Durham: N.C. Duke University Press, 1997, p.423.
11. *National Assembly of Pakistan Debates,* March 15, 1966, Karachi : Government of Pakistan Press, 1966, p.496.
12. Salman Taseer, *Bhutto : A Political Biography*, New Delhi : Vikas, 1980, p.145.
13. Ashok Kapur, *Pakistan's Nuclear Developments*, London : Croom Helm, 1987, p.137.
14. "N-option open if security threatened: Musharraf", *The Dawn*, 5 January, 2002.

15. Devdutt, "Indo-Pak Confrontation", *Young Indian* (Weekly), January 5-11, 2002, p.3.
16. Quoted in *ibid.*
17. C.Raja Mohan, "Fernandes unveils 'limited war' doctrine", *The Hindu*, 25 January, 2000.
18. "Pakistan must give back PoK : PM", *The Tribune*, Chandigarh, 18 February, 2000.
19. See Palmer, *Op.cit.*, p.409
20. See Callard, *Op.cit.*, p.317 *et. al.*
21. Wilcox, *Op.cit.*, p.97
22. Nazir Hussain, "India and Pakistan : Threat Perception & Prospects for Nuclear Risk Reduction", *Regional Studies*, Islamabad, Vol. XIX, No.2, p.68.
23. Vijay K. Nair, "The structure of an Indian Nuclear Deterrent", in Amitabh Mattoo (ed.) *India's Nuclear Deterrent : Pokhran II and Beyond*, New Delhi : Har-Anand, 1999, p.68.
24. R.V.Misra, "India's Image in the Indian Ocean : Need for better Projection", *Vikrant*, New Delhi, Vol.III, No.2 (August 1982), p.40.
25. Hussain,*Op.cit.*, p.62.
26. As reported in Editorial, "Gloomy Scene", *The Hindustan Times* (Patna), August 18, 1999.
27. Ayaz Amir, "Pakistan wants Peace and a little flexibility on Kashmir", *Young Indian* (weekly) July 7-13, 2001, p.8.

APPENDIX

INDIA-PAKISTAN : COMBAT STRENGTH

INDIA		PAKISTAN	
Total Army	: 11.75 lakhs	Total Army	: 5.87 lakhs
Main Battle Tanks	: 4500	Main Battle Tank	: 2120
Artillery	: 4175	Artillery	: 1590
Bombers	: 772	Bombers	: 410
Aircraft Carrier	: 1	Aircraft Carrier	: 0
Submarine	: 19	Submarine	: 9
MISSILES		MISSILES	
Prithvi	: 150-350 km.	Hatf-I	: 60-100 km
Agni-I	: 1500 km	Hatf-III	: 280 km
Agni-II	: 2100 km	Shaheen-I	: 750 km
		Shaheen-II	: 2000 km

Source : Devdutt, "Indo-Pak Confrontation", *Young Indian* (weekly) January 5-11, 2002, p.4

4

INDO-PAK RELATIONS: Lessons In Cooperation

Indra Mohan Jha

At the root of the Indo-Pakistan conflict lies the ideological divide between the advocates and opponents of the two-nation theory. In simple terms the two-nation theory argues that: Hindus and Muslims are two separate and distinct nationalities which can only survive in two different independent nation-states. The divide remains unresolved even after more than fifty years of their "separate" existence. One of its consequences is that each refers its neighbour as "Hindu India" and "Muslim Pakistan". The two phrases are not merely descriptive but one of hate and contempt.

For Indians, Pakistan was a country born in betrayal, while Pakistanis perceived their separate nation as liberation from perpetual Hindu domination over whom they ruled for centuries. Many Indian nationalists including Sardar Patel, J. B. Kripalani and Jawaharlal Nehru openly claimed that Pakistan would collapse because it was not a viable state. Circumstances would force the constituent parts—East & West Pakistan, both of which seceded to form Pakistan would return back ultimately to the fold.[1] Since independence many Indians had been predicting Pakistan's fragmentation. The birth of Bangladesh added substance to this fragmentation thesis. Memories of partition and later developments have created conditions for mutually reinforcing strange kind of mutual insecurity.

In this paper I shall argue that the two-nation theory continues to influence relations between India and Pakistan. Diplomatic negotiations and efforts for bilateral cooperation have only limited role to create conducive conditions for reconciliation of clashing interests for mutual benefits. Agreements on the Indus water and the Rann of Kutch are some useful examples of cooperation based on commonality of interest. However, these endeavours in cooperation could not take India and Pakistan in the direction of enduring peace and amity due to increasing consolidation of communal politics with its violent manifestations on both sides of the border.

The dilemma of Kashmir is perhaps the best expression of this India-Pakistan insecurity. The hostility over the status of Kashmir has led to three open wars and several border skirmishes. Until the mutual insecurity in the sub-continent is not addressed, Kashmir will not only continue to fester but remain irresolvable. In this regard it is important to mention Mountbatten - Jinnah talk in Lahore on November 1,1947. In this conversation, which took place three months after independence, lies the seed of allegations against one another continuing till date. Jinnah expressed his anger by saying that:

> the accession was not a bona fide one since it rested on "fraud and violence" and would never be accepted by Pakistan... this accession was the end of a long intrigue and that it had been brought about by violence... I (Mountbatten) countered this by saying that I entirely agreed that the accession had been brought about by violence,... the violence had come form tribes for whom Pakistan was responsible— Jinnah repeatedly made it clear that in his opinion it was India who had committed this violence by sending her troops into

> Srinagar;.... At the end Jinnah became extremely pessimistic and said it was quite clear that the Dominion of India was on to throttle and choke the Dominion of Pakistan at birth, and that if they continued with their oppression there would be nothing for it but to face the consequences. He was not afraid; for the situation was already so bad that there was little that could happen to make it worse...[2]

These perceptions of domination, betrayal, existential insecurities have lingered on the psyche of leaders and people of the sub-continent. Periodic manipulation of religion and propaganda accentuated to national apprehensions, India's overarching and predominant power always seemed as a threat to Pakistan. Internal disturbances in both the countries had cross-border connections and spill-over effects. India's midwifery of Bangladesh's birth and Pakistan's wars against India along with Pakistani proxy wars in the Punjab and Kashmir and insurgent group in North-east made these hostile perceptions more rigid. Naturally, both the countries often vowed to destroy other's existence as their goals. So-called Hindu nationalists in India proclaimed to reinvent and re-establish *Akhand/Vishal Bharat* by incorporating the erstwhile parts of the British India. In Pakistan the dominant policy remains to capture Kashmir and balkanize India to assert its existence against "expansionist Hindu India". This *Jihadi* zeal becomes more strident particularly when the rulers of Pakistan are internally challenged.[3] Islam in Pakistan with its symbiotic relationship with its "perceived threat" from "Hindu India have buttressed communal feelings in the elemental passions of people in the country and contributed to Indo-Pakistani tensions.[4] Even nuclear bomb was given civilization colour by Zulfiquar Ali ..Butto in Pakistan[5]. Most adroit military ruler Zia-ul-Haq enforced this hostile two-nation theory as a clear state policy *vis-à-vis* India. He put ISI machinery under military officers who were either *Jamaat* sympathisers or shared Zia's religious fundamentalism and militant Pak nationalism. It was to "achieve Zia's declared goals to establish fundamentalist Pakistani satellite regime in Kabul and to destabilize Kashmir and Punjab".[6]

Pakistan always viewed India as a powerful big bully. India saw Pakistan capable of creating internal disturbances. For both the neighbours this proved historically true. This mutual threat perception is fed on troubled elites by internal insecurity. Separatism of various kinds are rampant as the processes of national integration and nation-building remain colossal incomplete tasks. Doubt, distrust and uncertainties have incited and encouraged religious fundamentalism; which in turn create endemic socio-economic and cultural conflicts. These factors have diminished their national unity and self-confidence. Both will move ahead of this situation only by reliving of unwarranted fears of their neighbours and themselves. Therefore, Indo-Pak relations would not improve unless nation-building creates two sound and self-assured nations guided by secular politics. However, this requires enlightened leadership with modern mind-set and new ideas setting aside old myths of their religious nationalism to fashion new national priorities.

Therefore, the so-called core issue of Kashmir should be perceived from new perspective and approach. Neither India nor Pakistan can have whole Kashmir by force. Secondly, the Pakistani dream of an Islamic state has been realized even without insertion of "K" in their name. India must re-evaluate the Nehruvian thesis that the loss of Kashmir meant the demise of secular democracy in India. It would appear valid only if Pakistan succeeded in conquering whole of Kashmir. This seems impossible as both the countries are nuclearised. Nevertheless, the significance of Kashmir has been blown out of proportion by both the countries. Following facts justify this argument :

> The importance of Kashmir has been frequently exaggerated. It is of only secondary military significance in the Indo-Pak confrontation, for the military threat to each nation lies across the endless plains of the Punjab, not the narrow valleys of Kashmir. The

> annexation of Indian Kashmir by Pakistan would not automatically make Pakistan secure, nor would it increase her strength. Indian control over the entire territory would accomplish little more in regard to Pakistan than to cut off some potential invasion routes into the valley. Politically both capitals (New Delhi and Islamabad) argue that Kashmir is essential for national unity. But Pakistan's drive for the mountain state had increased the country's disunity by alienating East Pakistan and there is no evidence that the central Indian government is too weak to survive the separatist pressures that night follow relinquishment of Indian Kashmir. Rather Kashmir is the symbol of the broader military, political and religious insecurities of the two adversaries; it has become a convenient peg on which to anchor world attention and to base internal propaganda. An equitable solution would not effect the wider Indo-Pak problems, except to create an atmosphere of goodwill. But progress towards easing basic Indo-Pak differences might well relegate Kashmir to the secondary position.[7]

Thus, it is clear that the so called " core issue" of Kashmir is not so important for the survival of either India or Pakistan. Instead both the countries have bled white in conflict over Kashmir since independence. Both ruined their economies by diverting scarce resources for armament and creating hate for the other purely in religious terms to crush "Hindu India" or "Muslim Pakistan." Their hostility compelled them to accept subservient positions in the global power politics. Hostility with India drove Pakistan to American military alliance system and to counter that India joined hands with the USSR, compromising its policy of non-alignment. Both paid heavily in terms of their international relations and diplomatic manoeuverability. Trivial issues have made them suffer, this is exemplified by costs of recent troops deployment along Indo-Pak borders. About Rs. 8000 crores have been spent on deployment and withdrawal of Indian forces along the Pakistani borders in eight months (December 2001 to October 2002).[8] Almost similar amount must have been spent by Pakistan for the same. Has deployment served its purpose? The same amounts could have been used to change the fate of the poorest of the poor in the sub-continent. However, both the countries are involved in a perennial internecine struggle that has proved self-defeating in every respect. Obsession with Kashmir has distorted their foreign policies and poisoned their politics. Actually, Kashmir is the peak of differences, and must be approached by clearing away the undergrowth at its base. Positive ideas should constantly be produced for the improvement of relations between the two countries to the point where in a climate of understanding and good neighborliness the dispute in Kashmir could be seen in its proper perspective.[9] Proper perspective may be evolved by honest and sincere initiatives by India and genuinely reciprocated by Pakistan by adhering to the following suggestions:

(a) Strict adherence to the principle of pacific settlement of disputes;
(b) Promotion of communal harmony and secularization of polity;
(c) Free flow of people and information;
(d) Promotion of bilateral trade and commerce; and
(e) To establish mutually beneficial joint projects having equal stakes for both the countries.

Amidst conflict, cooperation between Indian and Pakistan is often glossed over. Both the countries also have some experiences of solving crucial problems by negotiation and building bridges of cooperation having equal benefit in their continuation, In this regard, the examples of the Rann of Kutch and the Indus water treaty are of immense importance.

RANN OF KUTCH

The Princely Kutch state merged into India on May 4, 1948

by signing Instrument of Accession. Pakistan raised the question of the exact location and demarcation between the Kutch (India) and Sindh (Pakistan) border. It is 320 miles long and 50 miles wide area which is virtually an uninhabited marshland. During half the year the area is covered with water. Oil deposits are reported there, but never exploited. Unless they exist, the Rann is economically and strategically useless. Nevertheless India and Pakistan have quarreled periodically over the status of an irregularly shaped portion of the wasteland totaling about 3500 sq. miles. Pakistan claimed that the Rann of Kutch should be treated as an inland sea. Hence, the border should be in the middle of the Rann, that is along the 24th Parallel and claimed over a territory of 3500 sq. miles. Both the countries claimed the territory referring to different agreements, pre-partition gazetteers and maps in their favour.

The dispute was first considered in 1948 when some diplomatic notes were exchanged between the two countries. The matter was discussed between Sardar Swaran Singh and Lt. Gen, A.M. Sheikh in (4-11) January 1960 when border discussion took place at Lahore, Rawalpindi and Delhi. Four out of five disputes on the agenda of the meeting were resolved. Four were regarding the interpretation of the Radcliffe Award. About the fifth it was decided to "Collect further data in respect of the dispute regarding the Kutch/Sindh boundary, and discussions will be held later with a view to reaching a settlement of this dispute."[10] These negotiations failed to resolve the issue and in early 1965 Indian and Pakistani troops clashed in the area. However, India treated the Rann adventure of Pakistan as a "test to gauge the mood of the Indian army. It was the precursor of, and preliminary to, the more ambitious operations scheduled some four months later when the Kashmir conflict opened." [11] For whatever was the motive behind, immediate cause of conflict was border dispute in the Rann of Kutch.

However, the belligerents realized dangers of escalation and at the initiative of the British Prime Minister Harold Wilson a settlement was formalized between Lal Bahadur Shastri and Ayub

Khan during the Commonwealth conference in London in June. The agreement signed on June 30, 1965, provided for a cease-fire and restoration of the *status quo ante* as of January 1, 1965 in the Rann of Kutch. Article 3(i) provided for negotiation between the two governments for the determination and demarcation of the boundary, failing which the matter would be referred to an international tribunal of three members. Both India and Pakistan were to nominate one member each and jointly select the chairman. If both fail to agree on the name of the Chairman, the U.N. Secretary-General would nominate the same. Moreover, the decision of the tribunal was to be binding and could not be questioned on any ground whatsoever.

Pakistan named Nasrollah Entezam, an Iranian diplomat and India named Ales Bebler, a judge of Yugoslavia. UN Secretary-General appointed Gunnar Lagergren, a Swedish judge as Chairman of the tribunal. The tribunal had 171 meetings. On 19 February 1968 its verdict was announced by a majority decision of two to one.[12] Pakistan was awarded about 350 sq. miles in the northern part of the disputed Rann and the rest remained with India. Thus, Pakistan got one tenth of its claim. Both the countries accepted the award with some objections raised by different sections. However, the significance of acceptance of an international tribunal and respecting of its awards shows determination of leadership to be above mob passions to settle bilateral disputes for peace and amity. Claims and counter-claims in Indo-Pak relations have led to wars, death and destruction. Rightly, tribunal chairman Lagergren referred to the complex nature of the dispute in which the respective claims and the evidence adduced in support of them in respect of certain parts of the disputed area was capable of being interpreted either way.[13]

INDUS WATERS DISPUTE

The drawing of boundary between India and Pakistan failed to take into consideration water distribution from the Indus canal system between India and Pakistan. The Indus river system consists of seven rivers-the Indus, a tributary on the west, the Kabul river and five tributaries on the east, Jhelam, Chenab, Ravi, Sutlej and Beas. Indus, Jhelam and Chenab flow primarily through Pakistan carrying about 80 percent of the waters of the Indus system. Ravi-Sutlej mainly and Beas wholly flow through India. Five of the six rivers have their upper reaches in India. These rivers are so linked with each other by a series of canals that in case there is shortage of water in one, a main link canal can draw water from another as it was conceived as a holistic system. Partition cut right across the system.

On April1, 1948, the Government of East Punjab cut off water supply to Pakistan on ground of non-payment of dues. As a result about 5.5 per cent of the cultivated area in Pakistan did not get water in the beginning of summer sowing season. Lahore's main source of municipal water was also cut off. This created furore in Pakistan. The representatives of both the countries signed an agreement on May 4, 1948; without finding any permanent solution. It only referred to that the "Governments of East and West Punjab are anxious that this question should be settled in the spirit of goodwill and friendship without prejudice to its legal rights; the East Punjab Government assured that it has no intention suddenly to with-hold water from the West Punjab, without giving it time to tap alternative sources". [14] Soon complaints from both the sides began to pour in. Bilateral meeting in Lahore and New Delhi in July 1948 and May 1949 failed to settle differences. Pakistan finally repudiated May 4, 1948 Agreement on August 23, 1950.

A new hope beaconed in the form of initiative by David Lillienthal. He was helped in this regard by Eugene Black of the World Bank. Their efforts resulted in an agreement on March 13,1952 that "so long as the cooperative work continues with the participation of the Bank, neither side shall take any action to diminish the supplies available to the other side for existing uses."[15] Thus began several rounds of talk, which ultimately culminated in the famous Indus

Water Treaty signed by Nehru and Ayub Khan in Karachi on September 19, 1960. The salient features of the treaty are as follows:

1. The waters of the Indus, Jhelum, and Chenab, except for essential uses in their own basins while they flow in India, are allotted to Pakistan and the waters of the Ravi, Beas, and Sutlej, except for a transition period during which Pakistan will build works to replace the waters received by it from these rivers, are allotted to India.
2. India has guaranteed to let flow for all time to come the waters of the Indus, Jhelum, and Chenab to Pakistan except for certain uses in Indian territory to be made in accordance with detailed regulations specified in the treaty.
3. India will continue to give water from the Sutlej, Beas, and Ravi allotted to her under the treaty to Pakistan during the transition period only and at a diminishing scale. The transition period will be 10 years. This period may be extended for a further period of three years, at Pakistan's request, but the extension is subject to reduction in the Indian contribution toward Pakistan's replacement works.
4. Pakistan has undertaken on the western rivers a comprehensive system of replacement-cum-development works comprising storage reservoirs, barrages link canals, tube-well drainage, and hydro-electric installations. As the purposes of part of these works is the replacement from the western rivers of water supplies for irrigation canals in Pakistan that were dependent on water supplies from the eastern rivers, India has agreed to make a fixed contribution of Rupees 83.3 crores toward the cost of replacing these works. The United States of America, Britain, Canada, West Germany, Australia, New Zealand and the World Bank are financing the remaining cost of this large plan of works. This arrangement falls outside the treaty. Their aid to Pakistan will aggregate to Rupees 333.3 crores. The United States and the World Bank have

agreed to lend India Rupees 26.7 crores for the construction of the Beas dam.

5. The treaty provides for a permanent Indus Commission to serve as a regular channel of communication on all matters relating to the implementation of the treaty.
6. The treaty also provides for neutral expert and a court of arbitration to settle disputes.
7. The treaty terminates the Indo-Pakistan Waters Agreement of 1948 under which canal waters were regulated from India to Pakistan until now.[16]

The Indus water treaty was an outstanding example of a cooperative endeavour between two countries to solve a very difficult and complicated problem satisfactorily; as Jawaharlal Nehru said at the time of signing the treaty in Karachi. He further added, "if we approach any problem in the world in a spirit of cooperative endeavourer, it will be much easier of solution than it might appear to be. I welcome the spirit, which in spite of all difficulties and obstructions and obstacles has triumphed in the end. Ultimately, the spirit does triumph—"[17]

The Indus water treaty and agreement on the Rann of Kutch are two important examples of the fact that if the leadership in both the countries work in a spirit of cooperation and long-term national interests, then even the most intractable problems might be solved by making mutual adjustments in their claims and position. Moreover, hawkish jingoism should not sway their vision. After all, even the Kutch and the Indus treaty were criticised is both the countries. Pakistan was unhappy by getting "The barest minimum of the essential areas" in the Kutch. In India some sections denounced it strongly. Jansangh leader Balraj Madhok described the Kutch award as the latest in a series of surrenders "before the enemies of the country at the cost of India's territorial integrity". Praja Socialist Party (PSP) leader Nath Pai called it a reward to Pakistan for its aggression against India. Madhu Limaye warned that Socialist Samaj

Party (SSP) would oppose it tooth and nail.[18] Likewise Nehru and Ayub Khan were criticized for signing the Indus treaty. Important Congress leaders like Morarji Desai and G.B. Pant had serious differences with Nehru. Ayub Khan was criticized by politicians, engineers and the bureaucrats. Fatima Jinnah, who opposed Ayub in 1964 elections, accused him to have sold Pakistan's waters to India.[19]

FUNCTIONAL APPROACH

On both the above issues the storm has settled. Both the countries have realized the significance of the two treaties. Moreover, the Indus canal treaty has bound the two neighbours in such a functional interdependence that even during the two wars (1965, 71) and later on during the Kargil skirmish no government ever threatened the Indus water system. The lack of mutual threat was only due to the functional importance of the Indus canal system for both India and Pakistan. Any damage to dams would have irreparably damaged both the countries. The message is clear: Indo-Pak hostility could be transformed into peace and amity only by organizing mutually beneficial joint ventures in different sectors such as, electricity, irrigation, tourism, health, education and culture. Mere political slogan of peaceful co-existence has failed them in the past and instead brought intermittent conflicts and wars. It is imperative to begin co-activity which would in turn lead to peaceful co-existence. People in India and Pakistan turn hysterical in the name of national pride and support war efforts. Since interaction and interdependence between the two is nil. Hence, empty calls of nationalism and sovereignty of their motherland and holy land tend to sway their emotions only to be expressed in terms of direct action against the other. However, creation of webs of functional units bringing benefits to peoples in streets would change their thinking to cooperation from conflict. The theory of functionalism in international affairs is based on following premise:

> Man can be weaned away from his loyalty to the nation ... state by the experience of fruitful international cooperation; ... beyond the level obtainable within the state... Individuals and groups could begin to learn the benefits of cooperation and would be increasingly involved in an international cooperative ethos, creating interdependencies, pushing for further integration, undermining the most important bases of the nation-state... the functional approach could eventually enmesh national governments in a dense network of interlocking ventures... the loyalty of citizens... would have been weakened in the development at the popular level of a social–psychological community which stressed super-ordinate cooperative goals.[20]

Co-activity thesis aims at creating a peaceful world "through doing things together in workshop and market places than by signing pacts in chancelleries".[21] In last fifty years Indo-Pak political leaders and diplomats have concentrated on conflictual issues to protect peace. They did little to work together in peace. That is why, they failed to promote and prolong peace. A working peace provides opportunity to "suffuse the world with a fertile mingling of common endeavour and achievement"[22] for a society geared to prosperity, welfare and justice. Conflict and war originate in their absence.

SAARC

The absence of endeavour for peoples welfare and justice is being filled by the organization called South Asia Association of Regional Cooperation (SAARC) though its gradual emergence was due to adverse prevailing political situations in South Asia. SAARC states may have divergent political, security and economic perspectives but they inhabit the poorest people in the world [23] having common desire to prosper, progress and develop. Therefore, the SAARC was conceived as a developmental regional organization by concentrating only on those sectors which bind them together in their quest for peace and development. The prime objective of the SAARC is to promote welfare of South Asian peoples and to improve their quality of life by bringing economic growth, social progress and cultural development with public participation. In a sense, SAARC was envisaged as a process of peoples movement so that the spill–over of cooperation may instil a sense of larger South Asianism instead of narrow nationalism. This is also manifested in crucial economic sector. Now, with more interaction among different sectors of people even Pakistani businessmen are eager to establish strong economic relations with India. There is far more unofficial and third party trade than official one between the two countries,[24] particularly in necessary commodities resulting in massive loss for both the people and business community. Even in hostile political scenario new business ideas are being innovated. Tyres and passenger cars cannot be officially traded between India and Pakistan. India's Ceat tyre company, therefore, set up a wholly owned subsidiary in Sri Lanka and now exports tyres to Pakistan. Toyota has set up a plant in Pakistan on the condition that it would export 50 per cent of production to India. Thus, political hostility and boundaries are being negated by economic gains. Rightly said Mohammad Naeem, Vice-president of Lahore Chamber of Commerce and Industry, " No government can compel businessmen not to trade when businessmen see there is money to be made."[25] Such a perceptive change in Pakistan is a welcome development for Indo-Pak relations because good trade makes good friends. Seeds of friendship are being sown at every level under the banner of the SAARC. Circles of cooperation have been created amongst peoples__ youth, artistes, academics, parliamentarians, businessmen etc. This new approach of peoples participation should be encouraged between India and Pakistan.

Managers of security and diplomacy are suspicious of their neighbour's designs and utterances due to their training, aptitude and inclinations. The Indian sub-continent was partitioned due to the two-nation state ideology proclaimed by the leaders of Muslim

League , foremost being Muhammad Ali Jinnah. The atmosphere continues to be vitiated by same elements having least concern for public welfare. They have used religion only to control the state apparatus. In this state-centric age even track-two diplomacy can be facilitated only by governments. Failed, unpopular and undemocratically geared regimes are opposed to cross-border public goodwill. Instead they have often indulged in generating hatred to garner sustenance for their regimes. Political elites in India and Pakistan are engrossed with *domesticity in their behaviour by taking narrower view of their interests. Domesticity refers to excessive influence of immediate domestic issues on foreign policy decision–making and diplomatic behaviour for short-term domestic gains* calculated in terms of increase in support base for the ruling elite.

In all likelihood, this desire to create political support base, at any rate, has played havoc with the life of peoples in India and Pakistan. Indo-Pak bashing is a routine ritual during elections in both the countries. It has no real substance. It is only a hate campaign based on two–nation theory. Jinnah was well aware of the dangers of the two-nation theory and knew well the significance of secular society for development. Therefore, he took a U-turn after creating Pakistan. He transformed himself once again into the old ambassador of Hindu-Muslim unity when he said:

> "you are free; you are free to go to your temples, you are free to go to your mosques in this state of Pakistan ——you may belong to any religion or caste or creed – that has nothing to do with the business of the state. We are starting with this fundamental principle that we are all citizens and equal citizens of one state."[26]

The ultimate truth of a secular democracy could not take root in Pakistan for the logical process which Jinnah started was undemocratic and communal. Naturally, Pakistan turned into a fundamentalist Islamic state and in India, Gandhi–Nehruvian secularism got skewed by self-seeking politicians. Thus, the two poor countries joined hands in mad arms race and later nuclearised to destroy one another. And even the conduct of diplomacy is based on scoring over one another merely to bring false cheers for their domestic constituencies. This kind of diplomacy with slogan-shouting and sabers-rattling has earned South Asia the sobriquet of being one of the most dangerous regions in the world.

It is high time that leaders and people of the two countries believe that use of force cannot achieve anything. Wars bring miseries even for victors and peace showers prosperity on the vanquished as well. India's midwifery in the birth of Bangladesh did not reduce Pakistan's capacity to trouble India; instead Bangladesh proved another Pakistan for India. Likewise, Pakistan must realize that its proxy wars even with rattling of nuclear missiles cannot destabilize India.

Kashmir, too, cannot be totally integrated into India by force, nor Pakistan can capture it by wars. This is clear from hard bitter experience. Only peaceful and friendly relations with more interactions in markets and work places can produce an environment conducive to equitable and just solution to the Kashmir problem. However, at the moment it seems difficult due to the rising tide of ideology *Hindutva*. Modi vs. Musharraf in the Gujarat assembly elections (2002) symbolised bilateral fundamentalism flattering the ego of the votaries of the two-nation theory on both sides of the border. In such a scenario any number of talks (Lahore or Agra) would produce simply more Kargils.

A new approach in this new age must be tried. This calls for an active role of rational elements in both the countries to evolve ways and means for increased cooperation amongst businessmen, players, singers, academia and media persons. Larger the number of peoples in workshops, markets, playgrounds, theatres, seminars and symposia; less would be left to uphold the culture of bayonets and bullets. Nevertheless, both the countries should give up diplomacy by propaganda obsessed with mutual hate campaign swayed by mob mentality. One can be tough, blunt and confrontationist as far as foreign policy is concerned, but in diplomacy one must be mild, hopefully optimistic and nuanced..... Diplomacy is the only way out in most difficult situations.[27] Mediatory efforts, facilitatory modes of negotiations aided and assisted by friendly nations and organizations would make it easier to resolve even sensitive issue like Kashmir. However, this would not be possible until we rationalize our thought process and realize that due to our shared history, shared geo-political realities and similar socio-economic situations, we are like the Siamese twins, one cannot hurt the other without destroying oneself. To put it other way, peace and prosperity in India and Pakistan cannot be achieved unless both work together in this direction. At the moment, it seems a distant dream but, only those who dream and hope can bring revolutionary change.

REFERENCES :

1. Michael Brecher, *Nehru: A Political Biography* (London: Oxford University Press, 1959), pp. 377-78.
2. November 7, 1947, *Mountbatten's Personal Report,* p.343 and 347. cited in Stanley Wolpert, *Jinnah of Pakistan* (Delhi : Oxford University Press, 1984), pp. 352-53.
3. See, David Taylor, "The Politics of Islam and Islamisation in Pakistan," in James P. Piscaton, ed. *Islam in the Political Process* (Cambridge: Cambridge Univ. Press,1983); Saeed Shafaat, "Politics of Islamisation : The Ideological Debate on Pakistan's Political System," *Asian Profile* (Hong Kong), vol.15, no.5, October 1987 pp. 445-58.
4. Aswini K. Ray, "Myths in American and Pakistani Foreign Policies: Their Contemporary Relevance", *Foreign Affairs Reports* (New Delhi), vol. 29, nos. 9-10, September – October 1980, p. 193.
5. Bhutto proclaimed in *If I am Assassinated* (Vikas,1979), "we know that Israel and South Africa have full nuclear capability, The Christian, Jewish and Hindu Civilisations have this

capability. The communist powers also possess it. Only the Islamic civilisation was without it, but that position was about to change".

6. Selig S. Harrison, "South Asia and the United States: A Chance for a Fresh Start", *Current History* (Philadelphia, Pa.,), vol. 91, no. 563, March 1992, p 97. These goals were told by Zia to the author in a conversation in Islamabad on 29 June 1988, as claimed.
7. Russell Brines, *The Indo-Pakistani-Conflict* (London: Pall Mall Press, 1968), p.436.
8. *Hindu* (New Delhi), 27 October 2002
9. Russell Brines, n.7, p. 436.
10. *Keesing's Contemporary Archives* (London), 1960, p.17262.
11. D.R. Mankekar, *Twenty-Two Fateful Days: Pakistan Cut to Size* (Bombay: Manaktalas, 1967), p.17.
12. Indian nominee Bebler cast a dissenting vote, observing that the boundary lay along the northern edge of the Rann, according to MacDonald's Survey 1855-70. This was shown in all later maps of the British India.
13. Cited in Farzana Khan, "The Rann of Kutch Award," in V.Grover and R. Arora, ed., *50 Years of Indo-Pak Relations* (New Delhi: Deep & Deep Publication, 1998), p., 82
14. Cited in Hafeez-ur-Rahman Khan, "Indo-Pakistan Waters Dispute", in Grover and Arora, n. 13, p. 21
15. Cited in Ibid, p.23.
16. See The *Indus Waters Treaty* (Karachi), 19 September 1960.
17. Jawaharlal Nehru, *India's Foreign Policy : Selected Speeches, September 1946-April 1961* (New Delhi: Publications Division, 1971), p.482.
18. See Farzana Khan, "The Rann of Kutch Award", in Grover and Arora, ed., n.13, pp-82-84.

19. See M. Rahman, *Divided Kashmir* (Boulder. L. R. Pubs. 1996), p. 176.

20 Paul Taylor, "Introduction", in David Mitrany, *The Functional Theory of Politics* (London: Martin Robertson & Co., 1975), P.x.

21. David Mitrany, *A working peace System* (Chicago: Quadrangle Books, 1966), p.55.

22. Ibid. p.98.

23. Amongst South Asian countries only the Maldives (84th), Sri Lanka (89th) and India (124th) fall in medium category of HDI and the rest are in low HDI, such as Pakistan (138th), Bhutan (140th), Nepal (142nd) Bangladesh (145th), See *Human Development Report* (New York: O.U.P.), 2002.

24. Third-party and unofficial trade shares have gone more than $ 2.5 billion.

25. See *Time of India* (New Delhi), 14 and 23 December 1995.

26. Stanley Wolpert, n. 2, p. 339.

27. A.K. Damodaran, *Beyond Autonomy: Roots of India's Foreign Policy* (Bombay: Somaiya, 2000), p.9.

5

Indo-Pak Strained Relations

Jayant Umranikar

The history of Indo-Pak conflict is similar to a story of two brothers, who had to separate because of the family feud over ancestral property. In this case, the divergence between the elites of two communities over the two- nations theory, religion, secularism and the world view, resulted in the division of the mother land. The tension between India and Pakistan has continued since then as the seeds of the present conflict were sown at the time of partition and pre-partition. Pakistan's hostile attitude towards India is mainly the result of the failure of Pakistan leadership to fulfill promises made to the Muslims at the time of partition .

The people of Pakistan and India share common history of over 5000 years. They come from the same background, have the same colonial experience and more or less, the same culture. Yet, India has done universally better than Pakistan. The latter's predicament is somewhat like the younger brother who parted in a hurry and anger from the elder brother but is now, envious and embarrassed by the progress made by his elder brother. Hence, in the name of Kashmir, 'the unfinished agenda of partition', Pakistan has been willing to cut its own nose to spite the face of India, initially by offering itself as a pawning great power-politics and now practicing terrorism as a state policy against India. This is an attempt to undermine India politically and economically, since Pakistan knows that it can never dominate the neighbor.

The strained relations between the two countries can be contributed to many factors:

1. DIFFERENT PATHS TO FREEDOM STRUGGLE.

Pre-partition Muslim League (ML) had developed on elitist lines while the Indian National Congress was a singularly popular, mass based movement. Hence, after the partition, the ML leaders like Jinnah, Liaqat Ali Khan or Surhawardy found that only the elite ML leadership had migrated to the newly formed nation, Pakistan, while their political constituency i.e. majority Muslim population from Indian territory, did not follow them. The ML leaders having accomplished their goal of a separate homeland for Muslims gradually lost its influence in the new nation, Pakistan. In the political vacuum, the armed forces found a wonderful opportunity to be a key political player in the chessboard of politics. Besides, Jinnah's two- nations theory was based on minoritism and an undemocratic principle viz. trying to raise democratic minority to majority by splitting the polity (Bhutto-Yahya Empire repeated this historical mistake when they refused to make Mujeebur Rehman Prime Minister of Pakistan leading to emergence of Bangladesh). The elitism of ML leaders also prevented spread of grass-root democracy in Pakistan. Their authoritarianism weakened democratic institutions paving the way to a smooth transition from British style 'Governor-General' to 'Army Generals'.

Mohammad Ali Jinnah died a broken-hearted man over his failure to create a secular nation as well as failure to secure Kashmir. Liaquat Ali Khan was shot dead by unknown assassins while Surhawardy melted away politically. The migrant Indian Muslims till date remain 'Mohajirs' i.e. refugees, in Pakistan, the nation created for the Muslims.

Mahatma Gandhi's contribution to Indian democracy can not overemphasize. During the freedom struggle, the father of the nation demonstrated to the masses that even most powerful empire can be challenged and changed through mass based, non-violent agitations like, non-cooperation movement, boycott of foreign goods, hunger strikes, peaceful processions etc. The Indian masses have learnt this lesson well and hence India has enjoyed uninterrupted democracy since freedom. Armed insurgencies of a various kinds, socialist, regional, tribal, ethnic have all failed in India as we could ultimately assimilate the dissidents into our democratic experiment. On the other hand elitist and feudal approach of Pak Leaders and lack of mass contact made Muslim League redundant in Pakistan paving the way to military dictatorship, time and again.

2. SOCIETY

Punjab constitutes nearly 60% of present day Pakistan, remainder is made of NWFP, Baluchistan- both overwhelmingly tribal areas- and Sind. In the British imperial set-up the present territory of Pakistan was considered to be an ideal 'breeding ground for soldiers and horses'. Hence the British did not encourage land reforms. Nor did the new rulers of Pakistan. The society in Pakistan has remained very feudal and authoritarian in-attitude. There are a few families controlling the whole economy and feudal clans like *Jatois* or *Bhuttos* possess vast tracts of land running into thousands of acres, even today. Entrenched feudalism prevented land distribution after independence and even Zulfikar Ali Bhutto's popular socialism stopped short of land reforms. Though genuinely popular, Z. A. Bhutto was an autocrat at heart. Thus while Punjab and Sind remains feudal, Baluchistan, NWFP and FATA (Federal Administered Tribal Areas) continue to have tribal leadership even today.

Soviet intervention in Afghanistan led to the rise of Islamic fundamentalism and two decades of Afghan war added elements of religious extremism, as well an 'opium and gun culture' into already decaying Pak society. Whenever in power, Pakistan's armed forces tried to depoliticise the system, ultimately paving the way for the rise of religious parties to power in Pakistan.

In this background, the land reforms conducted by Indian leadership, nationalization of banks, rise of public sector, affirmative action programme for the Scheduled Castes/Scheduled Tribes as well as consensus on distributive justice and mild socialism (mixed economy) helped India to come out of feudalism. The historically oppressed classes in India have now assumed political importance and social responsibility. In spite of periodic aberrations most of the political parties in India remain committed to democracy and secularism.

3. ARMED FORCES

Since the days of Prime Minister Nehru, the Indian army has remained a highly professional, apolitical force. In spite of numerous wars fought with Pakistan and one with china; in spite of Nobel Prize winner Sir V.S. Naipaul's characterization of India as land of 'a million mutinies' in the form of various insurgencies and deployment of army to tackle civil unrest and terrorism, the Indian Armed Forces have never sought a higher political profile.

On the other hand, Pakistan army an off-shoot of Indian Armed Forces, has never lost the opportunity to capture political power since the political disarray following Jinnah's death and Liaquat Ali Khan's murder. The army emerged as the most modern, organized force that could seize power from weak political leadership in Pakistan at will. The streak of militarism in Pak society and claims of martial superiority over the 'Hindu Baniya' also contributed to the rise of Armed forces in Pak polity. The Pakistani army led the nation into various anti-Indian alliances during the cold war. So also Zulfikar Ali Bhutto and later Gen Zia-ul-Haq formed anti-India axis with China .Ge. Ziz-ul-Haq, son of a Mullah brought the influence of religion into the armed forces. There was a large scale infiltration of Jamiat-e-Islami and Jamat-e-Tulba cadres into Pak Armed Force. Invoking and raising war cry of Jehad in Afghanistan (later on, in

Kashmir). Gen. Zia undermined the professionalism of Pakistani Armed Forces. 'Jehadi Fi Sabilillah' became the war cry of Pak Armed Forces.Gen. Zia also experimented with Sikh extremism and separatism. Later on , his political and military successors tried to use 'Mujahiddeen' tactics, perfected in the Afghanistan war, against the Indian authorities in Jammu and Kashmir.

Today the Pak army controls not only Politics but even economy of Pakistan. Most of the heavy industries are part of the military-industrial complex. Major scientific achievements, like Pakistan's nuclear programme, are also being run by the armed forces. More than 100 officers of Pak Armed Forces, serving or retired, occupy prominent positions in various Ministries, Corporations and administration. Others have turned into politicians. Thus the Armed Forces have their finger in every pie.

4. INTER-SERVICE INTELLIGENCE

Inter-Service Intelligence (ISI) was originally formed by a British officer, Hawthorn in 1948. The ISI was modified by Gen, Zia-ul-Haq into a political instrument of strategic value. Zia-ul-Haq created a political department in the ISI. Later on ISI encouraged formation of a political coalition, Islami Jamhuri Ittehad to fight Benazir and Pakistan Political Party (PPP). The ISI has been medlling in the political as well as social life of Pakistan. It has many political 'achievements' to its credit including formation of MQM (Mohajir Qaumi Movement). MQM Haqiqi, Muttehida Majlis-e-Amal, the present ruling party.

The Indian were taken aback when Gen. Pervez Musharraf announced in advance that the recent elections in Jammu and Kashmir would be rigged. However, Pakistanis cannot think otherwise as all the elections in Pakistan, since fall of Zulfikar Ali Bhutto, have been successfully rigged by ISI

ISI has become a hydra-headed monster which is beyond the control of any one institution. Its primary charter of collection tactical and strategic military intelligence has long been forgotten. Today it functions like a parallel government. Suppressing political dissent at home and trying to achieve Pakistan's strategic objectives through the spread of terrorism abroad, have become the charter for ISI. Pakistan's experiment with the Taliban in Afghanistan, its support to Al- Qaida, Musharraf's flip-flop in Agra are all too recent for one to forget.

5. SEARCH FOR NEW IDENTITY

Even after 50 years of existence, Pakistan and its society are in search of a new identify. They suffer from schizophrenia; they will not forget the fact that India helped to create Bangladesh in 1971 but would simultaneously like Indians to forget that ML divided India in 1947. Pakistan today, objects when South Asian sub-continent is called 'Indian' sub-continent. They dislike the notion of 'Indian' Ocean. Zulfikar Ali Bhutto sought to give Pakistan's South West Asian identity. He borrowed Awami dress from Afghanistan and worked untiringly for the formation of OIC (Organization of Islamic Conference). He was also responsible for the formation anti-India axis with China. Zulfikar Ali Bhutto's attempt to take over leadership of Muslim world nearly succeeded when his successor led international *Jehad* against the Soviet Union in Afghanistan in 1979. However, these efforts boomeranged when Pakistan overplayed its hand and became the vanguard of international Islamic Terrorism. Today it stands isolated in view of its subordinate relationship with USA.

Pakistan's efforts to break with Indian culture and historical heritage have also come a cropper. Even today Indian music, films and culture are a great attraction to Pakistanis and vice-versa.

6. JUDICIARY

Although Qaid-e-Azam, Muhammed Ali Jinnah was an outstanding barrister himself, the turmoil in Pakistan and frequent army interventions presented the development and consolidation of Pak constitution. The present constitution was enacted during the resume of Zulfikar Ali Bhutto in 1973.However,within a few months of its promulgation, President Bhutto, suspended the fundamental rights guaranteed under this constitution and proceeded to arrest his political opponents. In Pakistan the constitution has been followed more in its breach than observance. In contrast, the founding fathers gave India the constitution that has sustained this nation since its inception. Besides the legal atrocities committed by the military rulers of Pakistan, their constitution is also subordinate to the tenets of Shariat.

In India the judiciary has always stood up to protect and safeguard the fundamental rights, enshrined in the constitution January 26, 1950. In a historical case, Allahabad High Court Judgement,1974 went to the extent of unseating the incumbent Prime Minister Indira Gandhi whose elections had been challenged by Raj Narayan. In contrast, Pakistan's judiciary compromised its paramountcy by adopting Doctrine of Necessity to justify various military interventions in the country. The latest avalanche to hit the constitution of Pakistan is the legal Framework Order promulgated by Gen. Pervez Musharraf.

CONCLUSION

The above discussion has avoided summarizing known events of historical importance between the two neighbors. It also does not offer any political comment on the traditional rivalry. However, this paper makes an effort to show that the strained Indo-Pak relations arise out of the clash ot two opposite politico-religious systems and divergent societies. The difference is as wide as chalk is from cheese. It will be simplistic to conclude that the problem of Jammu and Kashmir is at the root of Indo-Pak feud. The above analysis will confirm that Kashmir is only a symptom but the disease is 'the inherently flawed relationship.'

6

Indo-Pak Trade and Economic Relations

Anand P. Mavalankar

"Do you know, my son, with how little wisdom the world is governed?" – AXEL OXENSTIERNA, Swedish Statesman Writing To His Son, 1648

Since the partition of British India in 1947, the sovereign states of Pakistan and India have pursued political policies towards each other to maximize their respective "national interests."[1] One wonders if they have fundamentally reconsidered their overall policy-positions[2] in light of lessons learned from their armed conflicts in the past.[3] The contentious political issues between India and Pakistan have negatively affected the evolution of the South Asian Association for Regional Cooperation (SAARC) as a regional organization. Consequently, the question of the South Asian identity has not received proper and adequate attention among elites, political parties, political leaders, intellectuals and scholars in India and Pakistan.[4] It is generally acknowledged that the geo-political and geo-strategic dimensions of Indo-Pak relations continue to preoccupy the minds of policy-makers and politicians in both countries.[5] While acknowledging the predominance of such dimensions that shape Indo-Pak relations,[6] this paper aims to explore trade and economic dimensions[7] of Indo-Pak relations especially in the past two decades.

At the outset, we shall briefly outline the historical context of trade and economic relations between the two countries. Before specifying concrete issues of trade relations, we shall refer to the changing international political and economic environment of the post-Cold War World Order.[8] The nature of argument also includes factors and forces that are internal to the civil societies of India and Pakistan. In this analysis, we shall identify some key trends of trade and economic relations between the two countries. We shall also endeavour to identify problems that affect the bilateral trade and economic relationship.

In the concluding part of this paper, I shall summarize my overall argument and indicate directions for possible breakthrough in Indo-Pak trade and economic relations in the near future.

– I –

The history of trade and economic relations between India and Pakistan is marked by two contrasting sets of factors and forces at both 'unit' and 'system' levels of analysis.[9] Being politically a single entity during the British colonial rule, trade and economic ties among areas of the present-day India, Pakistan and Bangladesh constituted a vital part of such relations.[10] Clearly, there were disruptions in such ties in the wake of the British colonial rule. But there was undeniably a solid base among those regions to engage in trade and other economic relationships. Factors pertaining to 'Comparative Advantage' and forces relating to the evolution of market economy in the Indian sub-continent were clearly facilitating sets of factors and forces that were responsible for promoting trade relations.

Following the partition of British India, the mutually antagonistic political policies of both India and Pakistan[11] hampered the conventional trade flows between regions comprising the newly-independent sovereign states. The emergence of Bangladesh in 1971 as a distinct new sovereign state further contributed to the dwindling trade flows in those regions as well.

During the Cold War era,[12] both India and Pakistan found themselves in two competing political camps. Pakistan's alliance with the United States in the 1950s and early 1960s had distinct economic implications. Pakistan's trade relations with India over the years have weakened considerably.[13] A quick glance at Pakistan's trade relations with the rest of the world would show their exports and imports to the Gulf countries as well as some key allies of the United States in West Asia and Europe. The low priority given to India in its trade profile was understandable in the Cold War era, where Pakistan's close military ties and political contacts with America largely shaped Pakistan's foreign trade strategy.

In the present post-Cold War phase of international history, it becomes imperative on part of both India and Pakistan to acknowledge the wider political and economic significance of the demise of the Cold War between the two major powers of the post-war world order ¾ i.e., the United States of America and the former Soviet Union. As regards implications of the emerging world order, both neighbours of the Indian sub-continent need to move away from 'Geo-politics' strategic frame to 'Geo-economics'[14] game-plan. The nature and level of economic and other kinds of cooperation achieved by countries of Western, Central and Eastern Europe points towards a distinct vision of geo-economics i.e., European Economic Community and Comecon. Past animosities and political rivalries among European states witnessed during the Second World War (1939-45) are largely set aside; and they have embarked upon a visionary course of political and economic action across the European continent.

The suggestion in this paper for adopting a normative position in this regard by India and Pakistan in their trade and economic relations, however, needs to be examined against the ground-realities pertaining to bilateral economic and trade relations between the two South Asian geographically proximate neighbours. The next section of this paper focuses on the nature and content of bilateral trade and economic relations between the two countries in the past two decades.

– II –

Before attempting a brief profile of Indo-Pak trade relations in the past two decades, a few initial remarks by way of defining the analytical task at hand are in order. Being basically a student of politics, we are primarily concerned about the political economy of Indo-Pak trade in terms of its overall character and direction. It goes without saying that a whole range of trade and economic statistics pertaining to the two Asian neighbours would greatly strengthen the economic nature of argument to explain patterns and processes of bilateral trade relations. For the purposes of this paper, however, we have chosen to leave the most detailed and discrete statistics alone. Instead, the objective of this paper is to interpret and explain, if possible, the overall trend and direction of bilateral trade relations. In addition, we have not employed a great deal of empirical evidence by way of citing different kinds of primary sources to support the underlying argument of this paper. In a word, we have employed only select statistics and some relevant secondary sources in making our overall argument.

A BRIEF PROFILE OF INDO-PAK TRADE RELATIONS

Prior to Pakistan's and India's independence, the trade relations among regions comprising contemporary India and Pakistan were indeed vigorous in terms both the range and scale of trade in various goods and services. During British India, there was considerable exchange of goods and services among these regions.[15] The partition of India was followed by certain political biases and prejudices that were reflected in the reordering of trade relations between two countries that were in two different ideological camps. This aspect needs to be kept in view before outlining a brief profile of Indo-Pak relations since 1947.

For nearly two decades after Independence, India was a major trading partner for Pakistan ¾ over 40 percent of exports and 20 percent of imports were to and from India. But since the 1960s, there has been a steady decline in India's official share in Pakistan's total trade and is now less than 1 percent. This happened despite the increase in the list of freely importable items from 42 in 1975 to 601 in 1998.[16]

If one reviews trade statistics between India and Pakistan since 1996, the dismal scenario of Indo-Pak bilateral trade is quite obvious. The following table indicates some basic trade statistics in this regard:

Despite noticing an increase in bilateral trade in the 1990s, official bilateral trade in actual terms was merely Rs.702.09 crores for the period 1999-2000.

India's main exports to Pakistan include edible oil , spices, drugs, pharmaceuticals, dyes, rubber manufactured goods (except footwear), paints, plastic and linoleum products. On the other hand, Pakistan's main exports to India include rice, fruits and nuts, sugar, textiles, leather, cotton raw and waste, etc.

As per one estimate, the official trade between India and Pakistan is roughly 200 million US $ dollars and the non-official trade approximates one billion US $ dollars.[18] The main reason for the flourishing of non-official trade is linked to Pakistan's refusal to buy certain Indian goods directly from India. Such goods include medicines, videotapes, viscose fibre, cosmetics, alcoholic beverages, cotton fabrics etc., which are traded through third countries (they are exported from India to countries like Singapore and Dubai, from where they are imported by Pakistan). Despite being imported through third countries, the Pakistani traders find Indian goods relatively cheaper. In addition, illegal trade between the two countries are conducted across the border. Goods traded illegally include cement, tyres, tea and chemicals.

From the Table indicated above, it is deduced that the bilateral

Indo-Pak Bilateral Trade Since 1996 (in Rs. Cores)[17]

Sr.No.	Year	Exports to Pakistan	Imports fromPakistan	Balance of Trade	Total Trade
1	1995-1996	257.00	150.09	+ 106.10	407.90
2	1996-1997	557.83	129.55	+ 428.28	687.38
3	1997-1998	537.83	139.68	+ 395.47	676.82
4	1998-1999	465.99	891.85	– 425.99	1357.84
5	1999-2000	405.35	296.74	+ 108.61	702.09

trade was less than 1 percent of their global trade. For example, during 1999-2000, Indo-Pak bilateral trade amounted to 0.22 percentage of India's global trade. Clearly, there has been very little of bilateral trade between the two countries. It is suggested that bilateral trade can be increased in items like tea, coffee, textile machinery and iron-ore. Presently, Pakistan purchases tea from Kenya at a higher price. Despite being the second largest consumer of tea in the world, Pakistan imports less than 2 percent of its tea from India. Similarly, the textile machinery industry in Pakistan imports material from Germany at a much higher cost. Further, Pakistan imports iron ore at higher cost from Australia and Brazil. Apart from the actual cost of iron ore, Pakistan has to pay a huge amount of freight and insurance for importing it from those far away countries. Instead, Pakistan could import iron ore and textile machinery at a much lower cost and insurance and freight charges would be considerably reduced. Above all, importing these items from India would make Pakistani goods such as steel and garments much cheaper, enabling Pakistan to compete effectively in selling their goods globally.

Another area of mutual gains for both India and Pakistan relates to gas reserves from Iran. In the last week of January 2003, this matter was discussed at the highest level by visiting Iranian President Khatami and the Indian Prime Minister, Vajpayee. Iran's huge gas reserves are a good prospect for India and negotiations have continued over the years. The sticking point, however, is India's reluctance to the gas pipeline being laid through Pakistan. As a matter of fact, the most economic way to transport the gas would be overland through Pakistan. It is understood that Pakistan is willing to be a part of such a deal, as it would be beneficial to Pakistan since it would earn approximately 500 million US $ dollars annually for the transit costs.[19] Further, the proposed pipeline would cater to Pakistan's gas needs during an emergency. However, India remains unconvinced with respect to the land route proposal and prefers a sea route at a much higher cost. India's objection to land route is based on security reasons, as India perceives that Pakistan could block the land route to hurt India economically in the event of a military conflict.

Still another matter of considerable importance between India and Pakistan is one of Pakistan according MFN (Most Favoured Nation) status to India. India accorded MFN status to Pakistan in the 1970s itself. Pakistan has so far not conferred the MFN status upon India. During the Delhi Round of Indo-Pak Talks - IV - on Trade and Commerce, Pakistan did not rule out the possibility of granting MFN status to India. Pakistan did not provide a time-frame for doing so. Pakistan's refusal of according MFN status to India can be attributed to economic and political reasons. Pakistan fears that granting such status would result in Indian goods flooding the Pakistani market, and Pakistani goods replaced by Indian goods. Consequently, the Pakistani authorities fear that it could have adverse impact on the domestic politics of Pakistan. Secondly, there is lack of political will on part of Pakistan to improve free bilateral trade relations with India. Pakistan fears that if the imports are liberalized from India, it might affect smaller industries in Pakistan which produce those goods.

The broad picture pertaining to the bilateral trade profile of India and Pakistan helps us in understanding the major areas of bilateral trade relations and the positions taken by India and Pakistan. It is necessary to look at both countries in terms of their interface with each other. The suggestion here is that it would enable us to focus on each country's overall economic status and gains that may accrue to them. To begin with, we shall analyze the trade scenario from the Pakistani viewpoint.

PAKISTAN'S TRADE SCENARIO

In the past decade (1993-2003), Pakistan's rate of growth has declined. It has faced a growing fiscal deficit, due to burgeoning foreign and domestic interest payment liabilities and defence expenditure.[20] So Pakistan has felt a compelling need to revive its domestic demand, accelerate industrial production and tap foreign markets to boost export earnings.

Keeping in view the state of the economy of Pakistan, it is suggested that greater trade-related exchange with India could bring in more export earnings for Pakistan. Relaxation of tensions between the two countries would restrict Pakistan's defence expenditure. Further, if Pakistan opens normal trade with India, it would be in a better position to earn a sizable amount by way of exports of goods (indicated earlier) to India.

It is interesting to note that in spite of the unresolved Kashmir dispute between India and Pakistan, large-scale unauthorized and circular trade continues to flourish between the two countries. This amounts to the loss of legitimate revenue for the government of Pakistan. Furthermore, restricting bilateral trade between the two countries has made Pakistan an artificially high-cost economy and has, in turn, deprived the consumers access to competitively priced commodities.

INDIA'S TRADE SCENARIO

India would definitely gain more if bilateral trade with Pakistan flourishes over time. The rationale for enhanced trade can be understood in terms of complementarities in the structure of the two economies, price advantages, low freight costs on account of contiguous land borders and cultural and linguistic similarities.

For both India and Pakistan, the agricultural sector remains the single largest source of employment. India can have increased business in food and agricultural products with Pakistan. As regards distinct advantages, Pakistan enjoys such advantages in electric power, cotton and textile production; while India enjoys advantages in engineering and household goods.

India has been importing sugar from various countries, including Pakistan. Pakistan has accused India in the past of obstructing sugar movement, especially by creating problems in unloading sugar in Amritsar. This causes a backlog, which adversely affects Pakistani traders. Further, there is a Pakistani charge on India for causing bureaucratic delays. India's stand regarding purchase of sugar from Pakistan is that the traders have freedom to buy sugar from any place where the prices are low and competitive. Further, sugar imports are on Open General Licence (OGL), so the question of delay does not arise. India's official view is that the delay is due to two factors ¾ (i) presently, only one train route between Amritsar and Lahore is available, which too is susceptible to fluctuating tenor of Indo-Pak relations and (ii) the use of outmoded rail wagons by Pakistan, which are not compatible with India's railway system.

PROSPECTS FOR EXPANSION OF BILATERAL TRADE UNDER SAARC

Since the establishment of the South Asian Association of Regional Cooperation (SAARC), in 1985 there is growing recognition of the potentialities of trade among all countries of the South Asian region. As two leading economies of the region, both India and Pakistan stand to gain from the South Asian Free Trade Area (SAFTA).

This, however, remains a distant dream, because both India and Pakistan are deadlocked over the Kashmir issue. Besides, resolving a number of security issues between the two countries would involve considerable long-term effort. Political compulsions for both India and Pakistan lead them towards stagnation in their mutual bilateral trade relations. Especially after the end of the Cold War (1989), most nations of the world have focused their foreign policies on the economic issues between and among countries and have considered prudent to improve their economic relationships with other countries to boost their own national economies. Some of the South East Asian Nations have embarked upon greater economic exchange among themselves, despite their bilateral political problems which culminated in the formation of a grouping called ASEAN in the year 1967.

The scope for cooperation under SAARC remains quite wide-ranging. If India and Pakistan cast aside their preconceived notions about each other, they could gain considerably as South Asian neighbours. They face the common problem of widespread poverty, illiteracy and severe demographic pressures. In order to solve it, both India and Pakistan need to raise substantially the rate of economic growth of their respective economies. Considerable increase in the export earnings through trade remains a crucial component in this regard. Both countries can gain substantially here if they have open, free and mutually beneficial trade relationship.

There are a number of areas where opportunities are available for both countries. In the area of agriculture and agro-business, there are products that both countries can buy from each other. Synergies in both bilateral and regional trade can be realized. As we indicated earlier, geographical proximity lends itself to lower transport cost and shorter transit time, leading to substantial benefits for India and Pakistan. Further, major commodities such as cotton, sugar, tea, wheat, rice and edible oil, provide numerous import or export trade possibilities. For example, as a regular importer of cotton, India can source a part of its requirement from Pakistan. Another commodity is that of wheat. Pakistan regularly imports wheat from countries other than India; while India always looks around to export its surplus wheat, which could be exported to Pakistan. Still another commodity widely consumed in Pakistan is tea. It is estimated that the per capita consumption of tea in Pakistan is almost double that of India's 600 grams and Pakistan is a regular importer of tea. Indian tea can find a good market in Pakistan.

On the basis of these commodities, both India and Pakistan can establish a genuine, mutually beneficial trade relationship. This, in turn, should help the process of confidence-building between India and Pakistan. Such a scenario should provide a more durable basis for cooperation among countries in South Asia.

OTHER DIMENSIONS OF INDO-PAK ECONOMIC RELATIONS

Apart from trade-related matters, we must analyze other dimensions of Indo-Pak economic relations. As one of the major dimensions, a brief word on monetary cooperation between India and Pakistan is in order. Exchange arrangements and exchange-rate systems are a sector wherein both countries can cooperate monetarily in both the short and long run.[21] In the South Asian context, a proposal for a common currency for South Asian countries would benefit both India and Pakistan in the long run. By reducing transactions and information costs, a single currency may encourage further trade amongst partners in a regional trade arrangement.

Another vital dimension of bilateral economic relations relates to greater movement of people of both countries through their respective land and air routes. Here the whole idea is to encourage visits of citizens of both countries, so that interaction among members of both civil societies is intensified. Visa procedures for businessmen should be simplified and made easier. Multiple entry visas and exemption from reporting to the local police are some other measures suggested to facilitate visits of citizens of both countries.

Another important matter relates to infrastructure, which is essential for bilateral trade. Both India and Pakistan should work towards the goal of free movement of goods by road, rail and sea. Trade by road between the two countries through Wagha border should be facilitated by mutually-agreed procedures of conducting such trade relations. Certain unreasonable procedures can be abolished in a phased manner. For instance, ships from Mumbai cannot empty its goods at Karachi unless it has touched a third country's port.

PROBLEMS FACING BILATERAL TRADE AND ECONOMIC RELATIONS

Despite the potential and promise of mutual gains from bilateral trade and economic relations, political compulsions in both countries dictate their foreign economic policies towards each other. Lack of trust and confidence between the two nuclear neighbours has, in fact, underlined the necessity of exploring avenues of mutual exchange and cooperation between the two countries.

The main political problem facing both neighbours in the Indian sub-continent relates to the collapse of diplomatic exchange between two governments. Since the Kargil War in 1999 between the two countries, summit-level talks between the Indian and Pakistani leaders in Lahore (1998) and Agra (2001) have not led to favourable conditions for genuine relaxation of tensions between them.

Normatively speaking, building trade and economic ties between the two countries would be effective confidence-building measures. But Pakistan's active support and training of terrorists and its policy of "cross-border terrorism" has made India's policy-makers unwilling to embark upon a meaningful trade policy with Pakistan. On the other hand, Pakistan's characterization of the Kashmir issue as "freedom struggle" and its active support to militancy in Kashmir has led to unifocal Pakistani foreign policy with India. Given the present state of Indo-Pak bilateral relations, the economic dimension of their relations continues to remain in the backburner of their overall policy-agendas. Whether a breakthrough in their relations can come about in the near future is a million-dollar question.

A BREAKTHROUGH IN TRADE AND ECONOMIC RELATIONS

Having reviewed the trade and economic relations between India and Pakistan, it is worthwhile to ponder over the question of a possible breakthrough in these relations in the near future in the new millennium. The point can be alternatively formulated by asking the question – under what conditions and circumstances a breakthrough in their relations can come about?

A few possible and provisional answers can be attempted here. First of all, the international political and security environment surrounding Pakistan may turn particularly critical and adverse towards it and may well force the rulers of Pakistan to change their ways in a fundamental sense. Pakistan, presently dubbed in some circles as 'epicentre' of international terrorism, will be increasingly isolated in the international community in view of its failure to eliminate terrorist groups within Pakistan and neutralize 'Jehadi' forces within Pakistan. The Pakistani military as a political institution will be, in all probability, faced with grave crisis of its own identity and credibility. Its goal of dismembering the Indian state with the help of Inter-Services Intelligence (ISI) and its mindset of destabilizing India are a source of considerable concern among the policy-makers of India as well as leading politicians and elites in the Western world. Given these considerations, the isolation of Pakistan as a 'rogue state' could generate a realignment of political forces within Pakistan. That may well create conditions for a breakthrough in establishing a more meaningful economic relationship with India.

Since the Kashmir elections in October, 2002 were held in a 'free' and 'fair' manner (as universally acknowledged), the stage is now set for political dialogue among all the concerned parties for a lasting settlement of the Kashmir problem. Though the process will necessarily take longer, it seems there will be a mutual sharing of views and a way forward could be carved out from the prevailing political situation in Kashmir.

Furthermore, numerous elites and citizens in both India and Pakistan have articulated and advocated a number of confidence-building and capability-enhancing measures to engage both societies in dialogue and collaboration in areas such as trade, cultural exchanges etc. Such voluntary non-governmental interactions between two societies would, in the long run, provide the basis for genuine bilateral economic and cultural relations between the two countries.

In the near future, a breakthrough in bilateral trade and economic relations can come about if the delegations of business leaders, intellectuals, artists, musicians, professionals etc. visiting these two countries (on a basis of mutual exchange) or such personalities visiting individually, could provide an actionable agenda on a number of matters of mutual benefit and gain. If these elites persuade and purposefully pressurize authorities of respective governments, new possibilities of cooperation and active collaboration would open up, especially in trade and economic area.

CONCLUSION

In this brief essay, we have endeavoured to analyze Indo-Pak trade and economic relations from a historical perspective. A brief profile of trade relations between the two countries is provided. While acknowledging the problems facing the turbulent and tension-ridden bilateral relations, the essay suggests that if political and diplomatic relations are handled wisely, we could expect a breakthrough in the near future in Indo-Pak trade relations.

REFERENCES :

1. On the question of 'national interest', the formulation of Hans Morgenthau with regard to 'national power' is quite useful in this regard. See his *Politics Among Nations: The Struggle for Power and Peace*, 5th ed. (New York: Knopf, 1973).
2. On overall policy positions of both countries, it is interesting to compare them in the wake of the armed conflicts and those made on a routine basis while conducting diplomatic relations between the two countries.
3. Here four specific armed conflicts between India and Pakistan include the 1947-48 tribal invasion, the 1965 Indo-Pak War, the 1971 Bangladesh War and the 1999 Kargil War. One wonders if appropriate lessons were learned by both countries in terms of ensuring long-term peace in the region.
4. The literature on the question of the South Asian identity

has been of recent times. It provides interesting insights into the inherent possibilities and potentialities for fostering cooperation among South Asian States.

5. In the last decade or so, memoirs and analyzes of retired diplomats as well as politicians involved in Indo-Pak relations provide useful information on the nature of bilateral relations.
6. Given the security dilemma faced by both states, one cannot simply ignore the geo-strategic dimensions.
7. The distinction between 'trade' and 'economic' dimensions is drawn to highlight the trade-related matters and indicate other non-trade-related economic matters.
8. The dissolution of the former Soviet Union and political change experienced by Central and East European States, as well as the lone superpower status enjoyed by the United States ¾ these changes have radically transformed the international environment.
9. The 'unit' level refers to that of sovereign states; while the 'system' level refers to the sovereign state-system as a whole.
10. This, indeed, is the original basis of South Asian identity cutting across the newly-created sovereign states in the Indian subcontinent.
11. The basis of these policies was influenced by superpower rivalries in the cold war era.
12. The military and strategic consequences of military alliance of Pakistan with the United States are indeed far-reaching in the evolution of strategic thinking and practice in the South Asian region.
13. Pakistan's close military and political relationship during that time led to considerable decline of Pakistan's economic ties with India during that time.
14. The game-plan of 'Geo-economics' can work in the South Asian region if two leading economies, India and Pakistan,

shed their current mindsets and embark upon a visionary course of economic development for both countries with commitment and unflinching cooperation.

15. Before 1947, in undivided India, surpluses in foodgrains, jute, cotton, spices, dry fruits and condiments were important exports from Pakistan. The Indian side, on the other hand, exported raw materials such as iron, coal and finished consumer products.

16. See Ashish Vachhani, "India, Pakistan and economic realism" in *Businessline*, 12 September 2001.

17. See Suba Chandran, Research Officer, IPCS, "Indo-Pak Trade" in article No.574, 12 September 2001.

18. See Suba Chandran, Research Officer, IPCS, "Indo-Pak Summit ¾ CBMs in the Economic Field" in *Businessline*, 12 September 2001.

19. See Suba Chandran, Research Officer, IPCS entitled "Indo-Pak Summit ¾ CBMs in the Economic Field" in *Businessline*.

20. According to the statistics of the State Bank of Pakistan, out of a total federal expenditure of Rs.77,000 crore in 1999-2000, Rs.31,360 crores was used to service domestic and foreign debt, Rs.15,250 crore was spent on the Defence establishment and in maintenance of internal law and order. Development-related activities, however, received a paltry Rs.1,900 crore. See Ashish Vachhani, "India, Pakistan and economic realism", (Mr. Vachhani is Deputy Secretary, Finance Department, Government of Tamilnadu).

21. See R.K. Madan, *Towards Monetary Cooperation in South Asia*. New Delhi: Concept, 1985.

7

INDO – PAK RELATIONS
A Case of Kargil Intrusion

Joseph Benjamin

In this paper an effort is made to study the origins of post- Partition 1947 aftermath which led to souring of relationship between India and Pakistan and climaxed in three open declared wars, several border skirmishes and Kargil intrusion. I would concentrate on Kargil stand-off in the crucible of its geographical terrain which shook and took by surprise India's political, defence, diplomatic and intelligence community. It was India's first television war, and public knowledge on security issues had escalated considerably.

ROOT OF INDO-PAK HOSTILE RELATIONS:

Indo-Pak Relation has been conflictual since the birth of two new independent nations on August 14-15, 19 47. To analyze the importance of Kargil intrusion, it would be essential to go back to the genesis of India's partition itself and further to the creation of more or less an independent state of Jammu and Kashmir during 19th century under the aegis of British Raj. The problem of Kashmir is a legacy of the partition of India in 1947 and an off-shoot of the lapse of doctrine of Paramountcy.

The communal division of India and Pakistan was basically engineered by the British to rule India though one can not overlook the fact of long standing Hindu-Muslim animosity. To separate two communities and to rule India through the much maligned ploy of divide and rule policy was in the minds of British since 1857. But the real partition was planned and nurtured since the end of the First World War. " The Communal partition was to create a north-west Islamic salient on the Indian sub-continent as a loyal rampart to protect the Middle East oilfields against a much feared Russian advance. Pakistan was thus a creation in their own interest." [1]. In the Independence Act July 18, 1947 the princes were free to execute an Instrument of Accession according to either Dominion under the Head of Defence. Lord Mountbatten the last Viceroy had a fixed mind that Kashmir should join Pakistan. He, in his top secret report, made it clear that he expected Kashmir to join Pakistan. In June 1947, he visited Srinagar and told the Maharaja that India would not object if he acceded to Pakistan, but Hari Singh evaded him .[2] Lord Ismay, during his visit to Kashmir also raised the issue of Kashmir, but Maharaja Hari Singh argued that "Kashmiri Muslims are different from Punjabi Muslims."[3]

During the time of tribal invasion which began on October 22, 1947, Maharaja Hari Singh appealed Indian assistance to solve this problem. India urged formal accession in order to ensure complete legal as well as moral basis for military intervention. The Maharaja signed the Instrument of Accession of October 26, 1947 and it was accepted by India when it received simultaneous endorsement and appeal for help from Sheikh Abdullah, the influential leader of National Conference.

Accepting the accession of the State of Jammu and Kashmir, Lord Mountbatten replied to Maharaja Hari Singh on October 27, 1947 thus :

> "In the special circumstances mentioned by your Highness, my Government (Indian Government) have decided to accept the accession of Kashmir State to the Dominion of India. It is my government's wish that, as soon as law and order has been restored in Kashmir and her soil cleared of the invaders, the question of the State's accession should be settled by a reference to the people. Meanwhile, in response of your Highness's appeal for Military aid, action has been taken today to send troops of the Indian Army to Kashmir to help your forces to defend your territory and to protect the lines, property and honour of your people." [4]

It was cleared from Mountbattens' reply that he was in favour of plebiscite. After Independence of Pakistan, there were series of attack on Indian Territory, including solid back-up support to tribal invasion in Kashmir on October 22, 1947 and thereafter, involvement of regular Pakistani soldiers in the military engagement. The question of Kashmir remained the core issue of half century old enemity. The question of plebiscite is being raised by Pakistan in almost all national and international fora. During the cold war period of superpowers rivalry, policy of alliance formation was one of the foreign policy goal of both Washington and Moscow. USA found Pakistan as a ready all in its South East Asia Treaty Organisation (SEATO), Central Treaty Organisation (CENTO) alliance system and it thereby got a foothold in South Asian region. Kashmir issue and its resolution and was not very high on the agenda of policy makers in Washington.

The events leading to the legal accession to India by the Maharaja of Jammu and Kashmir State, Maharaja Hari Singh had virtually nullified his Standstill Agreement with Pakistan on August 14, 1947. India had responded to Pakistan's designs on Kashmir with great speed which was necessary and so it could not get popular approval of people at large within the country. Witnessing the fast

changing scenario in Kashmir, Pakistan totally disregarding the standstill Agreement, cut-off essential supplies. The matter became worse and on October 22, 1947,

Pakistan unleashed tribal invasion on Kashmir State. Kashmir was saved in the nick of time as one Sikh of Indian Army landed by air at Srinagar on the morning of October, 27, 1947 and rushed to the outskirts of hard pressed Baramulla [5]. "Tribal invasion was basically a British idea to ensure that the strategically important Gilgit Agency area comprising the Hunza, Nagar and Chitral areas could be safely secured by Pakistan without attracting undue attention in keeping with the British visualization of their Great Game Compulsions"[6]. Tribal invasion was the first proxy war wagged by Pakistan after independence. Kashmir is not being the only main issue for tribal invasion. After tribal invasion there were other two major wars (1965 and 1971) between India and Pakistan. Besides these wars, Pakistan has been trying to distrupt the peace process in Kashmir.

BACKGROUND AND GEOGRAPHICAL LOCATION OF KARGIL

After narrating the context of India-Pakistan stalemate one finds Pakistan hurtling itself headlong on into Kargil misadventure. The geographical area is mountainous and so the terrain is hard rugged sparsely populated rugged, and military planners of Pakistan chose the area to nibble away some chunk of land falling within the Indian side of LOC. The Kargil sector extends 168 km along the LOC, stretching from the Kaobal Gali in the west to Chorbatla in the east. The LOC itself runs along with watershed from Kaobal Gali to Kaksar and then from Shangruti onwards to Chorbatla. This total distance of about 80 km. is glaciated and was unmanned by both side till the Pakistan intrusion on May1999.

It stretches southwards into the Zanskar range towards Padam, extending almost 230 km. Along this avenue there is a district infiltration route albeit a lengthy one to Kishtwar and Doda close to Umasila. Being Shia and Buddhist populated area, this avenue is an operational infiltration route has not been given much importance hitherto by Indian defence planners and military bigwigs. This lacuna underscores the importance of Kargil as its capture by an adversary would give a wide, encircling capability and a backdoor entry into the valley through the Great Himalayan range.

Along the LOC, there is glaciated and inhospitable terrain, which has below freezing point temperature making it very difficult for a lay person or soldier to pass through. This stretch is almost 80 km. Even Austria-made Kolflach snow shoes, very costly Gorfex high-altitude gear, Russian made stromeyer tents do not provide full-proof protection to the jawans from rigors and vagaries of nature.

This area was very difficult for any organized force to negotiate and control and as threat was not anticipated, it was left unprotected. Still New Delhi had kept 121 (1) Infanty Brigade to look after the Kargil sector. After 1972, the Brigade was placed under 3 Division based at Leh in Ledakh. The Kargil Brigade which provided the only line of communication found itself always on a limb facing up to Pakistan in the crucial area. The down playing of threat perception by New Delhi was mainly due to its China fixation and for which the 3rd Division was deployed. It was undergirded by another variable, and that was POK area posing no threat because of its terrain in military thinking and calculation because the positioning of 3 divisions was made in such a way that with its limited resources it had to square up to twin threats coming from two opposite direction at the same time i.e. Communist China and Pakistan from its POK area. At the same time, the activation of Siachen conflict in 1984 and subsequent development of roads and tracks over the years within POK had altered the situation gradually. So the ground reality was gradually becoming unfriendly for New Delhi.

The Dalunang intrusion was noticed in October 1987. It took place at a time when the Pakistani attempt had been foiled at Bilafond La in the Siachen area. Dalunang intrusion was on the Indian side which had somehow escaped attention. As the track and other communication approaches to Dalunang village was widely believed to have residual land mines as a fall -out of the 1971 operations the area was left unpatrolled. The 121 Brigade was thus forced to chance its place of deployment to the Dras-Kaksar Area.

The Dalunang intrusion of 1987 was a classic case of Pakistani soldiers crossing into LOC and India failed to resolve the issue in a firm manner which emboldened Islamabad to what Pakistan repeat such activity in 1999.

The Kargil intrusion did not begin in 1999 but it had its origins three years earlier. The Government of India taking cognizance of setbacks in the area set up a Kargil Review Committee which observed that "From 1997 onwards there was increased activity in this sector, marked by heavy artilley fire. The magnitude of these exchanges rose two-fold in 1997 and three-fold in 1998. In 1998, reports indicated training of an increasing number of militants in the Northern Area and the likelihood of their infiltration through the Mashkoh Valley ."[8]

It is also believed that the Kargil intrusion of 1999 was originally conceived during 1987. After Altaf Gauhar, who once upon a time was Information Secretary to President Ayub Khan wrote in the daily *Nation.*

> "......the Kargil intrusion .... was authorised by Gen Zia-ul-Hag in 1987. But at the final committee meeting where Gen Zia was to approve it, the then Foreign Minister, Gen (Retired) Sahibzada Yaqub Khan opposed it on the plea that as a former general, he knew that the posts that Pakistani soldiers would occupy were totally covered with snow almost throughout the year and it would be extremely difficult to have communication with them and meet their day to day needs. He said that some soldiers had died there and their bodies remained untraced so far"[9].

The academic and military question which always crops up during the discussion of Kargil misadventure is why after all Islamabad backed up infiltration policy in and around Kargil and for what military and diplomatic gains. The following discussion attempts to unravel the true reason of the skirmish.

Pakistan is an Islamic State and increasingly it transformed itself into a fundamentalist country. At the same time, we notice that in Pakistan, there are three segments of society viz, civil, military and religious fundamentalist. In order to continue ruling, the government in power try to divert attention from the snowballing internal crises of Pakistan. Sometime they create tension on the border to internationalize the Kashmir issue. This is done to pollute the minds of ordinary Pakistani citizens so that the army, political leader and bureaucracy can rule Pakistan without any dissent or hindrance.

It is said that the Kargil intrusion followed the sequential nuclear tests conducted by the two South Asian adversaries in May 1998.

It is also understood that the real reason for Kargil war lies in Pakistan's repeated failures to annex Jammu & Kashmir through full fledged conventional wars. During the Kargil war, Pakistan planned a big operation to strike the Indian army's center of gravity in the northen part of Kashmir. Its strategic aim was to internationalize the Kashmir issue. Besides this Pakistan had also specific objective for Kargil war. They are as follows.

1. "Choke the strategic road linking Srinagar with Leh and prevent vital supplies for the ensuing winter reaching Indians troops in Ladakh.
2. Occupy Dras and Kargil and open up the LOC issue.
3. Capture heights in Battalik and Turtok areas to initially sever the Southern Siachen Glacier, and later, choke access to both the northern and southern glaciers along the Nubra river, and force India to back down on Siachen.

4. Control the Mushkoh valley near Dras and use it as a major route for fresh infiltration.
5. Spread insurgency in Kargil district of Ladakh to ease the heat unleashed on military groups in the valley.
6. To bury the Simla Agreement by altering the LOC and bring the Kashmir issue back on international stage".[10]

It is said that the intrusion plan was reportedly the brain child of Pakistan's Chief of Army Staff (COAS) Gen. Pravez Musharraf and Lt. Gen. Mohammad Aziz, Chief of the General Staff (CGS). They obtained 'in Principle' concurrence, probably without any specifics, from Prime Minister, Nawaz Sharif. After direction to President Bill Clinton's point blank maintain the sanctity of LOC, the Sharif agreed to withdrew its troop. But still Kargil can be remembered as a very important landmark in Indo-Pak tension-ridden relations.

The Kargil war encompassed the area from Turtok in the north to Mushkoh valley in the south. The important sectors pertaining to the terrain are Turtok, Chorbat La, Batalik, Kargil, Kaksar, Dras and Mushkoh valley. Turtok lies on the Shyok river and has a population of about 1,500. Indian troops stationed at Turtok have to travel up to Leh from where they are transported across the 18, 380 ft. high Khardung La. Therefore, the route lies along the Shyok valley. Over 1/3 of the route to Turtok is the same as that for Siachen. Any Pakistani advance up to Shyok valley would put pressure on the flanks of Indian soldiers traversing the route to Siachen and make the 3,000 m. high. The area of Chorbat La is part of the Batalik sector for operational purposes. Batalik sector lies to the north of the Indus River. There very many important villages along the river from the east to the west. They are Dah, Garkhum, Urdas and Batalik on the Indian side. There are three major nullahs (streams) flowing south from the LOC broadly dissecting the sector. These three stream join the Indus at Batalik, Garkhun and Dah. Batalik's ridges are less steep from the Pakistani side, and this is advantageous for the intruders who attempt of breach the LOC and occupy heights at 16,000 to 18,000 ft. without their movement being noticed. On Indian side, these positions had to be approached from very steep height i.e. up to 12,000 ft.

Kargil town lies at the junction of Shingo and Suru rivers. If one goes on along the Shingo, one would come to the village of Gangam, Bielargo, Olthingthang and Marol. They all come on the Pakistani side of LOC and were used as logistics bases. Point 4151 dominates Kargil town. It is 4 km. North east of Kargil and about 3 km from the LOC on the Indian side. It is the key to the town's safety from the barrage of Pakistani guns. This height was captured by India in 1965 war, but was returned to Pakistan after the Tashkent agreement. Again it was captured in 1971 by Indian troops. Kaksar is a village which lies to the west of Kargil. It is situated on the Southern bank of the Shingo river. Point 5299 dominates Kaksar which is very close to LOC.

The Dras sector is dominated by the Tololing heights to the north and the Tiger Hills complex to the north-west. In between there is Sando Nullah. Tololing is on the Srinagar- Leh highway and one can monitor all the clandestine activities from this place. A road running along the Sando Nullah goes right up to Morpo La on the LOC. Beyond, on the Pakistan side, is the road to Gultari, one of their important bases. Road from Gultari lead to Faranshat in (POK) and on to Shaqma. From the Pak side the Mushkoh valley is reached through the 5,353 m. high altitude Marpola Pass. There is no other pass in the vicinity, hence, control of this pass is very vital otherwise it cuts off access to the Mushkoh valley. On the Western side, the Mushkoh valley empties itself through the Kaobal Gali and the Tillel valley into Gurais, Spurs from this vantage-point Tiger Hill dominate the Mushkoh valley.

MILITARY ENGAGEMENT AT KARGIL

The Kargil stand-off is one more milestone in long extended period of continuous failure to annex Jammu & Kashmir. Two conventional wars, fifteen years of intermittent fighting in Siachen and twelve years of low-intensity militancy had been the unfortunate experience of Pakistan vis-a-vis India.

The central plan of Kargil strategy was to launch a big operation to strike at the Indian army's nerve-center in the northern part of Kashmir. Again Pakistan thought of bringing back the Jammu & Kashmir issue as a center of Indo – Pak tumultuous relations. Further, Islamabad thought that by choking the road to Leh and by outflanking the Indian army it would gain territory and at one fell swoop it would make mincemeat of sanctity of both LOC and Simla agreement. To realize these goals Islamabad well crafted means were encouragement to infiltration and export of militancy.

Though Kargil stand-off had its genesis since the time of Zia-ul-Haq, but it got real momentum after Lahore Declaration. (February 22,1999) Pakistan decision to plunge into Kargil misadventure was to a great extent shaped and guided by India's domestic situation. The then Indian Prime Minister, Atal Bihari Vajpayee's government was weak as it had no overwhelming suport in Parliament and the shadow of fresh election was becoming large on the horizon. In this scenario, things began to hot up, and Islamabad's quick military move caught the Indian Army napping some time in March, 1999. Heavily armed Pakistan-backed intruders dug themselves in at heights of 16,000-18,000 ft. on the Indian side of the LOC along an 80 km. stretch north of Kargil. And in the first week of May they began pounding the strategic highway linking Srinagar and Leh.

The development of roads, tracks and helipads may well have been revamped with all thoroughness in 1997 and or 1998 as a part of normal military activity. Logistic requirements and artillery build-up commenced in 1997 and was completed in 1998. Pakistan artillery duel with its Indian counterpart was in full force during the period. This was further supplemented by reconnaissance parties which were sent to probe the soft areas of the opponent crossing over the year 1998 and stretching right up to February, 1999. The reconnaissance forays succeeded fairly well as it occupied ground on the Indian side.

In the backdrop of this breakthrough, it was now the turn of regular Pakistani troops to seize ground on the Indian side of the LOC from February 1999 and then it tapered off by April, 1999.

The three residents of Garkhan village were the first to discover the disturbing reality of Pakistani intrusion on the morning of 3 May. The well armed intruders had moved up some 5 km along the Jubar Langpa and they were clad in Pathan attire digging bunkers as per to the account given by one of the informant of the village..

On May, 6 eight soldiers of an Indian Army patrol accidentally stumbled on a camp of about ten Pak personnnel on the Kukarthang ridge in the Batalik sector and lost one soldier in an ambush. Taken by surprise at the audacity of Pakistani intruders the Indian Army patrol hastily called up for more reinforcement to gain more information and evict the infiltrators. Soldiers of a second patrol sent out the next day May 7 were injured in a Skirmish. The gravity of the situation became evident and in the mean while Defence Minister Mr. George Fernandes had been briefed by the army high command on May 6. The matter did not rest as again another Indian patrol stumbled on a camp set up on the Kukarthang ridge in the Batalik area. On May 9 a third patrol party was ambushed. Taking cognizance of the seriousness of this extensive intrusion Pak infiltrators, Government of India launched " Operation Vijay" with stated objective to evict the intruders out of the Indian territory. On May 9, Pakistani intruders established observations post to facilitate its artillery barrage on strategic stretch of Srinagar – Leh highway and settlements around Kargil and Dras on May 14 six men patrol party of 4 JAT led by Lt. Sauron Kalia went missing while patrolling in the Kaksar area. Their dead bodies were received back on June 9, and it was a gruesome sight to behold. To acquaint himself with the situation, Defence Minister George Fernandes accompanied by General Officer commanding in chief of Northern command, H.M. Khanna visited the area of fighting where he was briefed by 15 Corps Commander, Lt. General Krishna Pal. This updated information was shared by the Defence Minister with the Prime Minister so as to chalk out a fitting counter strategy.

By May 18, the Army had gunned down 52 heavily armed Pak soldiers and many other in different parts of areas. Some Pak solidiers were seen in the Mushkoh valley. So soon it became clear that these were regular Pakistani soldiers who have intruded and occupies ground on the Indian side of LOC. On May 21, one Canberra reconnaissance aircraft was hit by a surface to air missile but limped back safely to Srinagar. By May 23 it was very much clear that 600-800 Pak infiltrators were well entrenched in the Dras, Kargil and Batalik sectors. These incidents had an important fall out as in an important meeting between the Army Chief and the Prime Minister, it was decided that any necessary action has to be taken to evict the intruders. The military strategy was changed, as it was decided now to bring in the Indian Airforce to help out the Army in the common goal. On May 26, Indian Air force started air strikes in Kargil. The morning sorties of MIG-212, swing-wing MIG 27s and improvised MA-17 helicopter gunships from the airbase of Srinagar and Pathankot to strike two sub base camps of the intruders at Point 4590 near Dras.[11] Just before noon of the same day May 26 another round of air strikes took place in the Battalik area. That Pakistan had anticipated the Indian reaction, including the air strikes, is evident from the fact that its irregular soldiers were even equipped into surface to Air Missiles (SAMs) a weapon that has not figured in the Kashmir conflict so far.

The next day May 27 the IAF lost a MI-17 helicopter after a very successful attack on Tololing in the Dras sector. Intruders using a shoulder fired surface to air stinger missile hit the chopper when it veered close to their hideout. MI-17 helicopters were not used in the war zone thereafter. Five air personnel died in this incident. These were to be the last losses suffered by the IAF, and has a spokesman said on May 28, "We have been operating in a very self-restrained manner and using air power in confined and difficult terrain".[12]

The military engagement on land still continued with greater intensity . On May 26, an eighteen man patrol from Grenadiers unit ran into heavy concentration of infiltrators in the area of Tiger Hill. Suddenly, machine guns started firing from three sides. In this process of exchange of fire four Indian soldiers were killed.[13] On May 29, a company led by Maj. Adhikari attempted an assault in the Tololing area. But they were stopped just 15 meters before their objective. The intruders rained fire on the attacking troops and pushed the company back 30 m. and even a little more backwards.

The Government of India seeing that the contours of war is changing, decided to use another wing of its force i.e. Navy. Indian Navy employed its satellites, reconnaissance planes and other modes of intelligence gathering to monitor the movements of the Pakistan Navy. The Indian Navy came to know that Pakistani had alerted its Navy. The Indian Navy was placed under high alert; it moved its Eastern fleet to join the Western Fleet in the Arabian Sea and deployed its maritime surveillance capabilities. These naval maneuvers ensured that the Indian Navy quickly took a forward position, thus denying Pakistan the initiative. Even the Navy had to take its position in order to improvise and use its ground based assets such as the Jaguar fighter-bombers.

Pakistan was surprised by Indian Navy's deterrent deployment which was given code name (Operation Talwar) that bottled up the Pakistani fleet in Karachi. This objective was mainly achieved by showing a massive build-up in the Arabian sea. The navy was thus ready to impose a naval blockage of Pakistan's coastline in the event of war.

In the first week of June 1999 itself, the Pakistani Army shelled the Akhnur sector along the LOC. At the same time, intense engagements began along the Chorbatla-Turtok alignment, north-east of Batalik in Ladakh where key segments along the entire stretch of LOC were affected by varying degrees of firing. Shelling was also directed from various sectors Keran, Uri, Poonch and Naushera. On July 4 Nawaz Sharif who made a hurried visit to Washington to meet President Bill Clinton to seek a way out as he felt the noose was tightening around Pakistan's neck in Kargil. Two leaders immediately met at Blair House for across from the White House for three hours. In return, the only concession Nawaz Sharif could wrest from President Clinton was a promise that he would take "Personal interest" in expediting talks between Delhi and Islamabad. But the joint statement issued by Clinton and Sharif made it clear that it would be done "once the sanctity of the LOC has been fully restored".[14]

Sharif not only tried to have support on Kashmir issue from Washington but he also made a short visit to London on his way back to Islamabad to win support for his country. But he did not get much sympathy that he was expecting from British Prime Minister Tony Blair. His capitulation at Western capital provoked a furious political backlash in Pakistan. This was largely because the Pakistani Government in past two month had created an impression before the public that the Mujahideen had achieved significant victories and it would not back down under any Western pressure. Many political parties in Islamabad were not happy with Sharif's claim that US would help inter nationalizing the Kashmir issue. Many of them saw the joint statement as a surrender deed and even accused Sharif of treason and betraying the freedom struggle. "The nation will not forgive Sharif for the sell-out on Kargil", warned Munawwar Hussain, Secretary General of the Jamaat-I-Islami, which is closely linked to the Islamic militant groups fighting in Kashmir.[15]

Even the Chief of the newly formed United *Jihad* Council, Syed Salahuddin declared that "We will not put our guns down. We will continue to fight till the last drop of our blood." He added further that the Washington deal as "a conspiracy against the Kashmiri Freedom Struggle". Defence experts in Pakistan now believe that Sharif was made to pull out from Kargil. US General Anthony

Zinni's visit in the last week of June 1999 made it clear that Pakistani leaders will have to take concrete measures to defuse the tensed situation.

The announcement by Pakistani Chief of Army Staff General Parvez Musharraf that Sharif would meet Bill Clinton even before the Pakistani Foreign Ministry made it public, was evidence that the army was in step with the Prime Minister's actions. That impression was strengthened a day after Sharif's agreement with Clinton when Musharraf told the longest circulated Urdu daily *Jang* "There is total unanimity between the military and the Government on the Kargil situation"[16].

All these cleared the major doubt on whether Sharif would be able to carry the military along on his decision to pull out the Pakistani troops from Kargil Muslim League enjoyed a handsome majority in Pakistan and there was no threat to Sharif Government. Before Kargil War, Sharif had emerged as his nations most powerful civilian Prime Minister. Although his public esteem has considerably dipped since then, he still had the clout to push through the decision without fear of being ousted. Part of the reason why army was string along with Sharif was the steady reversed its troops had suffered in Kargil. The Indian army, by capturing vital peaks in this war, were Tiger Hill and Jubar heights from where the intruders had threatened the strategic Srinagar – Leh Highway, has successfully thwarted the Pakistani objective of isolating Ladakh from the Kashmir

Valley. By following a policy of finely tuned restraint and not crossing the LOC to strike back, the Vajpayee government won the diplomatic war with Pakistan's close allies like US, China, and others. With Pakistani precarious economy dependent on international financial institutions like World Bank and the International Monetary Fund from whom the release of $ 100 million tranche was necessary for the economy to remain afloat. If this was not forthcoming, then Sharif's option would narrow considerably. Given his express commitment to Clinton, whatever palatable twist the Prime Minister may give it before the nation. The military pull-out from Kargil seemed imminent.

CASUALTIES

The Defence Minister Mr. George Fernandes, in his written reply to a question in Lok Sabha, stated that the Indian Forces suffered the following casualties during 'Operation Vijay'. This table shows the Indian causalities under different headings.

Indian Casualties [17]

	Army	Air Force
1. Killed	519	5
2. Wounded	1,365	–
3. Missing	1	–

It is not only that Indian Soldiers were killed in Kargil War, but there was also Pakistani Casualties. There were various estimates of Pakistani Army casualties, based on published material in Pakistan and from Indian calculations also.[18]

Pakistani Casualties from Indian calculation

1.	Army killed	733
2.	Officers	71
3.	Special Services Group (SSGs)	68
4.	ISI	13

It would be worthwhile to have a look at the Military capability from a holistic perspective of both India as well Pakistan during the period 1997-1998.

Battle Equations

	India	Pakistan
Defence Expenditure	$ 10.4 billion	$ 3.7 billion
Army	9,30,000	5,20,00
Tank	3,314	2,120
Towed Artillery	4,175	1,590
Air Force	1,10,000	45,000
Combat Aircraft	777	429
Helicopters	34	20
Navy	55,000	22,000
Submarine	17	9
Destroyers	6	3
Frigates	18	8

Source : Military Balance 1997-98 appeared in *India Today* July 5, 1999.p.23.

It is estimated that cost of war for India has skyrocketed upto Rs. 15 crore per day.[19] It cost more than 8,000 crore for India to make Pakistan understand that it meant business. Reverse mobilization of the troops back to the barracks cost Rs. 3,000 crore. Nearly the entire border and areas around the line of control (LOC) were mined. It cost the Government Rs. 850 crore in giving compensation to civilians for any physical disability during the mobilization period.[20]

A review of the total cost incurred during the Kargil conflict gives one a full picture of costs and expenditure. The government claimed that the 74-day 'Operation Vijay' total cost was Rs, 1,894 crore. The total number of shells used for firing was 2.5 lakh and the total expense for it was Rs. 1000 crore. The defence spending exceeded allocations by Rs. 2,409 crore in 1999-2000. The bill for supplies bought from ordinance factories has risen from Rs. 3,876 crore in 2000-01 to Rs. 5,972 crore in 2001-02. A leading Indian weekly *India Today* has observed.

The effect of Kargil on defence spending has been significant. Capital expenditure increased from Rs. 12,631 crore in 1999-2000 to Rs. 21,411 for 2002-03. Revenue expenditure including wages, welfare and allowances, rose from Rs. 35,893 crore in 1999-2000 to Rs. 43,589 crore in 2002. "In the past three years, the Government poured in Rs. 1,11,461 crore in the defence budget Rs. 79,725 crore as revenue expenditure and Rs. 31,736 crore for new technology armaments and replenishment" [21].

MILITARY EXPENDITURE

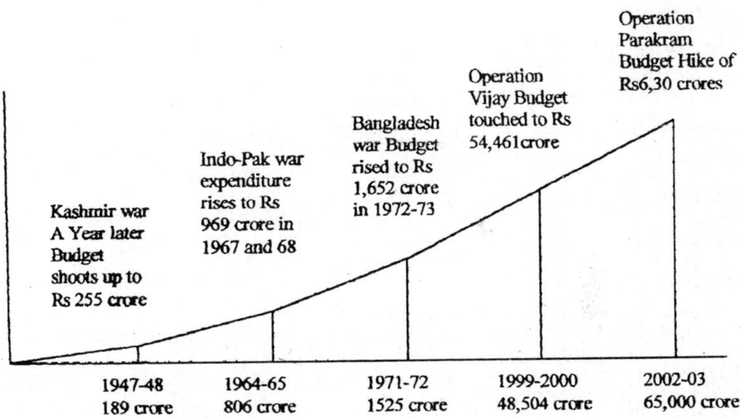

Source : *India Today* October 28, 2002. p. 22

This Graph shows how India has been spending on defence.

CONCLUSION :

Kashmir, the unresolved issue as Pakistan views it has led to many wars. Even this has led to nuclearization of two proximate neighbours. Three major wars (1948, 1965 and 1971) Kargil episode, India's military deployment on the borders after December 13, 2001, terrorist attack on Indian Parliament all cumulatively have kept the cup of embittered relations overflowing without any let-up. Again twice in the year 2002 in January and June India was on the range of war against Pakistan. Prime Minister Mr. Atal Bihari Vajpayee wanted to strike on POK-based terrorists, but Pakistan cleverly shifted their camps pre-empting Indian options. Government wanted limited action. The Military thought otherwise, saying the forces should cross the Indo-Pak borders. The leaders of Pakistan especially Zulfiquar Ali Bhutto's dreamt of attaining parity with India in nuclear field was realized in May 1998. General turned President Parvez Musharraf on January 4, 2000 stated that Pakistan would not hesitate to use nuclear weapons if its security was threatened. On January 24, 2000, while inaugurating an international conference on Asian Security in New Delhi, Defence Minister Mr. George Fernandes had declared "India's readiness to fight any limited conventional war under the nuclear shadow." [22]

This all shows that war cloud is still hovering on the horizon of both the countries. There had been open and proxy wars between two countries India and Pakistan. Both India and Pakistan should take a concrete step to resolve the dispute and inaugurate a new chapter of co-operation and to solve the much deferred domestic social problem.

A serious effect should be made by both the countries who are geographically proximate, yet have acted as distant neighbours. The first fall out should be serious pruning of bloated defence budgets and the ruling elites of both the countries should divert the funds for socio-economic development of toiling masses who suffer from endemic poverty, malnutrition, illiteracy and backwardness of all sorts. Even outstanding economists, social thinkers, intellectuals politicians, human rights activists have been harping on this theme unremittingly since long time. And to top it well-meaning friends in both India and Pakistan and all across the world. India spends on its defence just 2.8% from its Gross Domestic Product, while Pakistan significantly spends 4.8% from its GDP. Much of its defence allocation is used by Islamabad in prosecuting a low intensity conflict against India.

It become obvious that military expenditure is draining both the poor nations and one random examples speaks a lot. It costs Rs. 10 crore a day to maintain troops along the LOC to prevent another Kargil. Over and above this other hefty financial outlay has to be made for hinterland security. And this applies to Pakistan too.

In order to ease the tension a process of on-going dialogue and confidence-building measures should be encouraged. We have many examples from history that war cannot bring peace, and it applies to Indian sub-continent as well. Both India and Pakistan should come to the negotiating table and discuss their mutual problems. Both the governments should be people friendly irrespective of the divide of religion, caste, language etc. Kashmir is the part and parcel of Indian Union and it cannot be given to Pakistan under any circumstances. Even if Kashmir is given to Pakistan, whether Pakistan would ever stop terrorist activities in India is million dollar question.

REFERENCES :

1. Narendra Singh Saria "Kashmir and the Great Game: Pawn in West's Anti-Soviet Strategy". *Times of India*, 14 August, 2000.
2. D. Suba Chandran, "Why Kargil? Pakistan's Objectives and Motivation", in Maj. Gen. Ashok Krishna, and P.R. Chari, ed. *Kargil The Tables Turned* (New Delhi: Manohar, 2001) p.29.
3. Narendra Singh Saria op. cit.,
4. Jagmohan, *My Frozen Turbulence in Kashmir* (Nelhi; Allied Publishers), 1991, p. 86
5. Maj. Gen. Ashok Kalyan Verma, Kargil: *Blood on the snow.* (New Delhi : Manohar, 2002), p.37.

6. Ibid. p. 37
7. Ibid. p. 87
8. Kargil Review Committee, headed by Shri. K. Subrahmanyam was set up on 29 July 1999 and it submitted its report to the Union Government on 15 December 1999. The Report was tabled in Parliament on 24 February, 2000.
9. Altaf Gauhar, "Four Wars, One Assumption" *Nation* 5 September 1999.
10. Maj. Gen. Ashok Krishna and P.R. Chari op. cit. p. 98.
11. Manoj Joshi. "Blasting Peace". *India Today* 7 July 1999.
12. Maj. Gen. Ashok Krishna and P.R. Chari op. cit., p.107.
13. Ibid;
14. "Face-saving Retreat" *India Today* 19, July 1999/p. 21.
15. Ibid. p. 22
16. Ibid p. 23
17. *The Hindu*. 3 December 1999
18. Maj. Gen. Ashok Krishna and P.R. Chari op.cit. p. 137.
19. *India Today* 14, June 1999 p. 23.
20. Shankar Aiyar, "Wages of War". *India Today* 28 October 2002, p.22
21. Ibid: p. 23
22. C. Raja Mohan, "Fernandes Unveils Limited War Doctrine". *The Hindu* 25 January 2000.

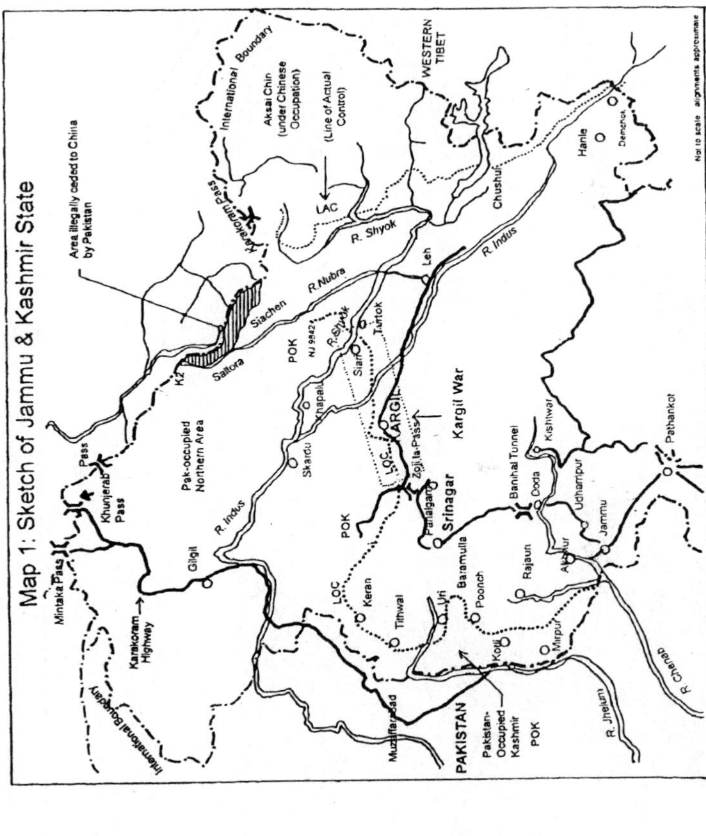

Source : Major General Ashok Kalyan Verma, Kargil, Blood on the Snow : (New Delhi, Manohar, 2002)

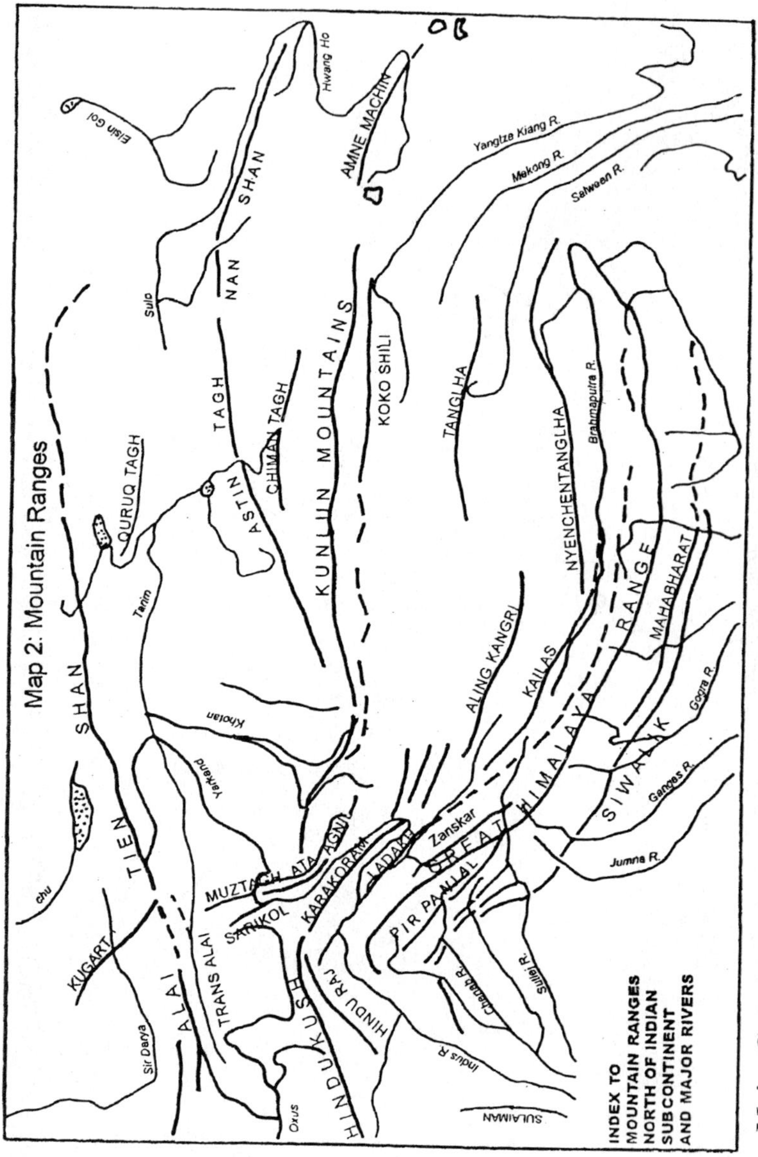

Source : Major General Ashok Kalyan Verma, "Kargil: Blood on the Snow" : (New Delhi, Manohar, 2002)

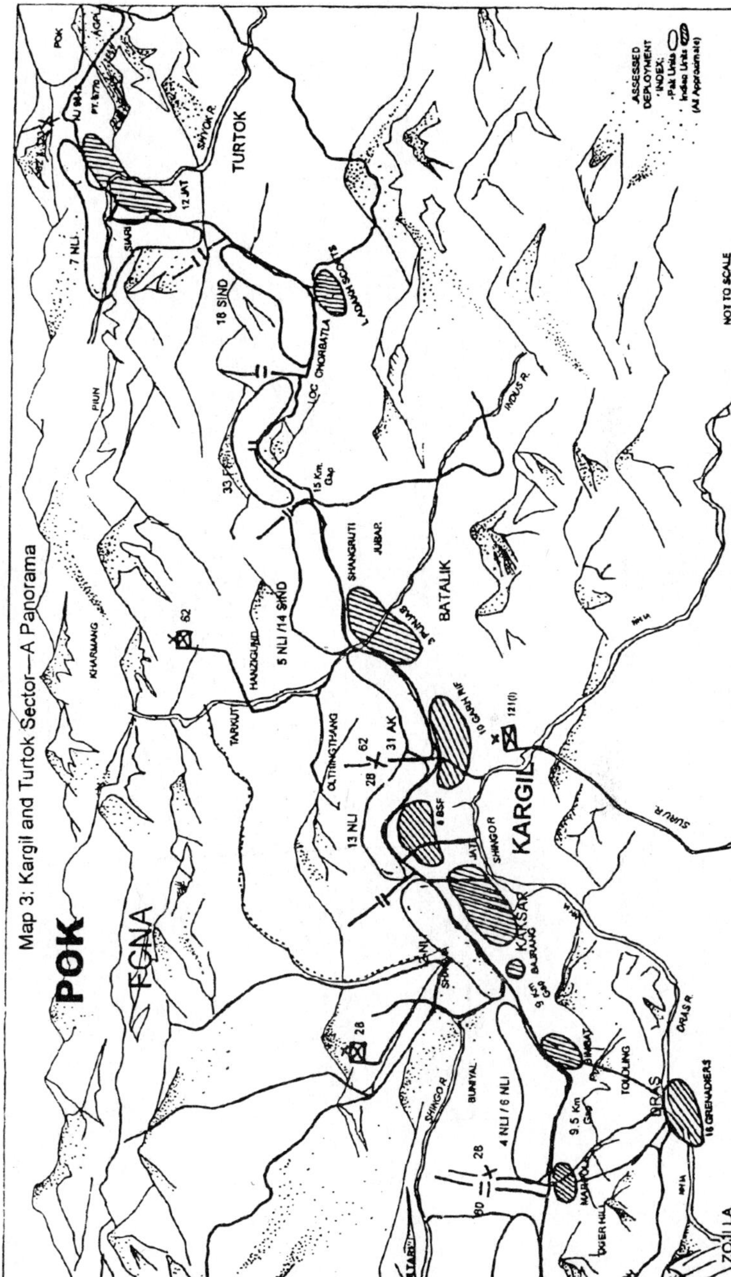

Map 3: Kargil and Turtok Sector—A Panorama

Source : Ibid.

Map 4: Kargil Intrusions (Mashkoh-Dras-Kaksar)

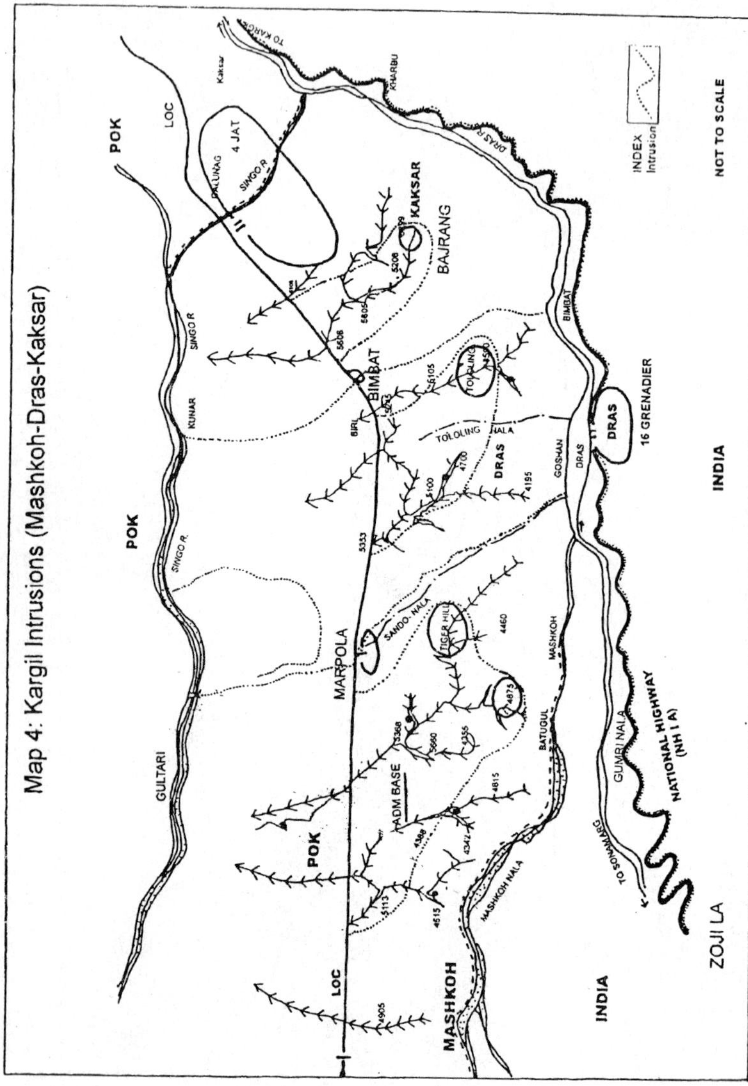

Source : Ibid.

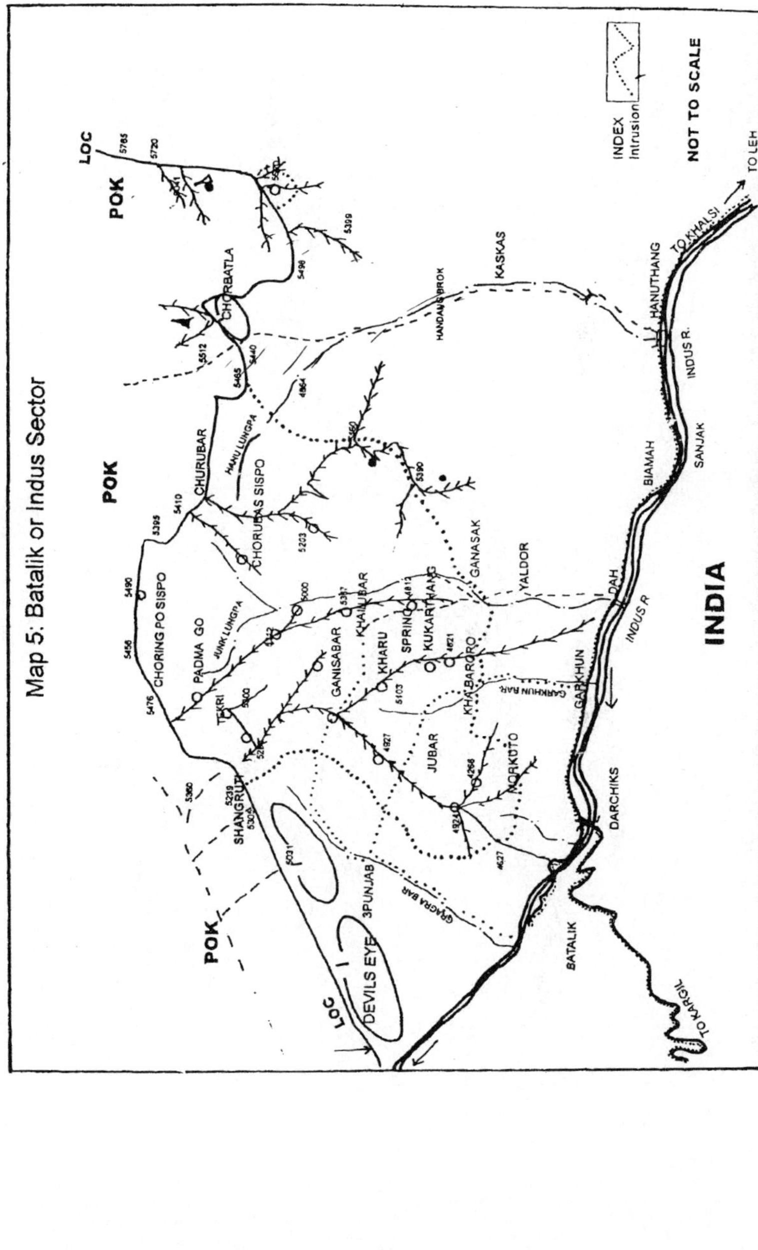

Map 5: Batalik or Indus Sector

Source : Ibid.

Map 6: Turtok Sector: Subsector Haneef (SSH)—Southern Glacier (SG)

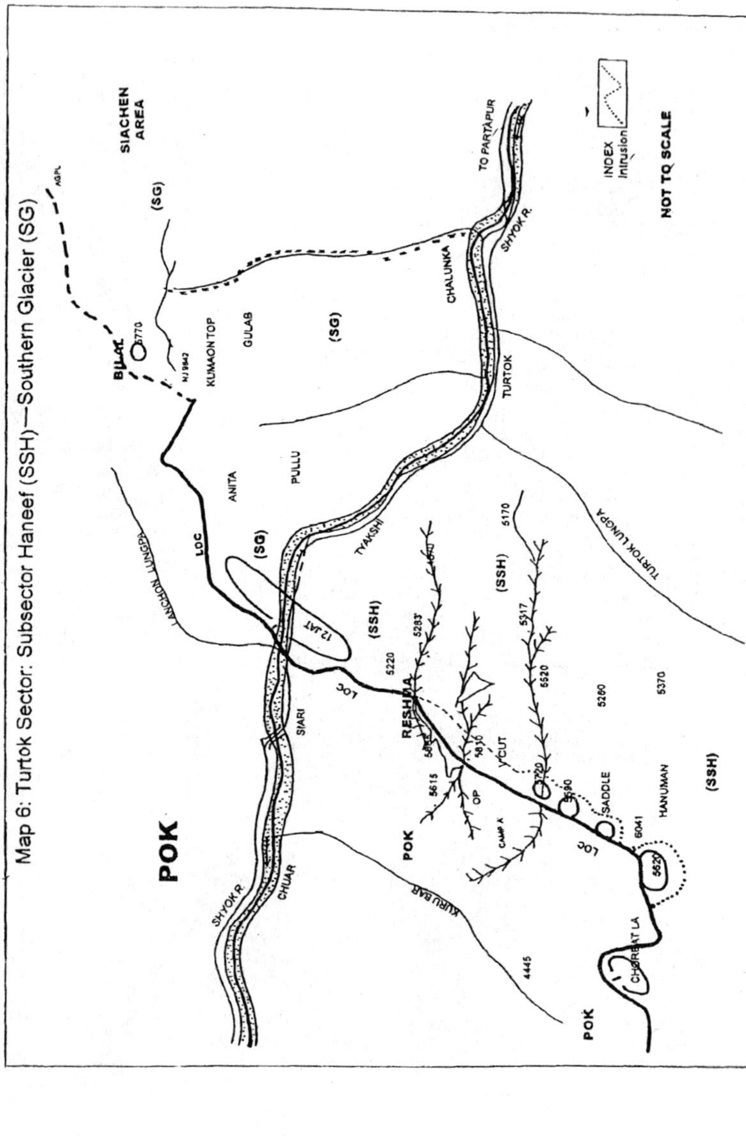

Source : Ibid.

Source : India Today, August 16, 1999, p. 48.

Source : India Today, July 5, 1999, P. 28.

8

SAARC and Indo-Pak Relations

Mohan Kashikar

Relations between India and Pakistan have always been a center of focus and most crucial aspect of foreign policies of both the countries. Indo-Pak relations have always proceeded on a bumpy ride. It has become a matter of global concern at the turn of the millennium, because the tension between the two countries has increased manifold. Some global events also focused the world attention on these two countries. This paper tries to analyze the basis of Indo-Pak relations and its conflictual nature, trace the working of the SAARC and finally evaluate the impact of SAARC on Indo-Pak relations and vice versa.

It is often said that SAARC is a hostage to Indo-Pak relations. Strained relations between these two countries have always affected the functioning of SAARC. Postponement of 11th SAARC Summit at Kathmandu and again the present standoff between India & Pakistan that has resulted in the postponement of 12th SAARC Summit, which was to be held in Islamabad in December 2002, are considered to be the latest major setbacks in the working of the SAARC. There is no doubt that the relations between the two have been coloured by the partition of the subcontinent in 1947 and subsequent violence, bitterness, hatred, mistrust and continuous flaring up of religious sentiments. The burden of the past weighs heavily on the leaders of the two countries. The colonial mind-set still persists. The post-1947 relations between India and Pakistan are just like an extension of the relationship that existed between Indian National Congress and the Muslim League before partition.

Here let me add that the fault lies with both. Pakistan and India have tackled the situation from different perspectives and followed strategies that suited their own national interests. None of them ever bothered to take a broad perspective or a regional perspective. Nehru tried to achieve some sort of regional cooperation in the 50s, but his experiments were for the larger Asian solidarity. Some of his initial over-enthusiastic statements, actions did create an image of 'Big Brother India'. Inexperience, extreme idealism and lack of diplomatic tactfulness of the leaders added to the complications.

For Pakistan, the relationship with India is based on a fear-psychosis; a fear that since India has not accepted partition willingly it will retaliate and finish Pakistan any time. The mindset of Pakistan has been explained in different terms like schizophrenia, Indo-phobia etc. According to one British scholar, Keith Callard, "Three factors are responsible to keep Pakistan intact or to be precise useful for the survival of the leaders in Pakistan – "Islam, Jinnah and Hate India Syndrome."[1] Premature death of Jinnah deprived Pak of one of its strong unifying factor. Islam served the purpose of creating Pak and so it lost its purpose as a unifying factor as its futility was proved beyond doubt when it could not withhold East and West Pakistan together and in 1971 Bangladesh was created. Besides Islam in Pak society presents a heterogeneous picture, full of number of sects and racial and ethnic groups who do not have congenial relations amongst them. So Islam also proved to be ineffective. Thus only one factor remained i.e: "Hate-India Syndrome!" So we see that India became a central theme in Pak's foreign as well as domestic policy. Everything in Pakistan is related to India. Pak desperately tried to achieve parity with India in every field. Pakistan raised the issue of Kashmir and claims that the agenda of partition is still incomplete. There were allegations and counter-allegation from both sides. Pak accuses India over Kashmir and also suspects that India is supporting Jiye Sindh Movement in Pak. India has blamed Pak for cross border infiltration and support to terrorist activities. There is not an iota of truth in Pak's allegations about India, but India's charges about Pakistan have been based on hard facts brought to light by our intelligence agencies and which are even supported by the US and British intelligence agencies. So Pak's involvement in terrorist activities in India is direct and proved beyond doubt.

All this has resulted into strained relations between India and Pakistan, but definitely affected the political situation in South Asian region also. Efforts of Nehru to achieve a regional platform did not succeed. All the South Asian countries were skeptical about India. Indo-Pak conflict and actual wars between the two in 1965 and 1971had its impact on the region as well. That is the reason why South Asian leaders had to wait till 1985 to form SAARC. When other regions of the world were already far ahead of South Asia in experimenting with the idea of a regional organization, South Asian leaders were fighting with each other. Importance of a regional organization dawned upon the South Asian Leaders very late. There were international compulsions, which led them to think differently. The South Asian leaders realized that the UN is not delivering significantly to the most underdeveloped areas of the world. Other agencies like the IMF, the World Bank have become tools in the hands of developed countries. Movements like NAM, Commonwealth were mere talking shops or clubs without any constructive or tangible outcome. Disparities between the developed and undeveloped nations were widening. And lastly the successful working of the regional organizations like the EU, ASEAN etc, impressed the South Asian leaders.

But more than these global factors there were domestic compulsions and compulsions within the South Asian region itself that enthused the leaders to think about forming a regional association. These compulsions were geographical, economic, cultural, educational, social and so on. South Asian region is in many ways an extended version of Indian subcontinent. In other words the region is "Indo-centric". All the features present in India can be seen all over the region also. These constitute the commonalities in South Asia:-

(a) Geographically SA is one single unit. All the countries are geographically contiguous and all the six share borders with India. Weather conditions in the region, Flora & Fauna, Vegetation, Forests, Condition of soil, Food habits are identical and shaped by the geography. So Geography has sealed their fate permanently.

(b) Common Economic Problems: Poor Agriculture, Planning, Poverty, Illiteracy, Housing, Human Resources, Population Explosion, Trade Deficit, External debt, etc.

(c) Religious Affinity – Presence of all religions, Sacred places all over the region.

(d) Social background – Language, Literature, Arts, Music, Social habits, Food habits.

(e) Common history and experience of colonial rule.

(f) World issues and common approaches thereon in international fora.[2]

These factors look like "Unity in Diversity". But unfortunately only diversities were highlighted all the time and all ignored the commonalities. So once the leaders realized these commonalities and internal compulsions then the process to have a regional organization began and ultimately SAARC was born in 1985.

INDIA'S POSITION

The question of Indo-Pak relations is highly complex. However, so far as India's policy towards Pakistan is concerned, it needs to be mentioned here that, notwithstanding the extreme anguish at the partition of their country, India did make earnest efforts to create good neighbourly relations with Pakistan. As early as on 22 December 1949, India proposed a no-war declaration to Pakistan pledging resolve to settle all disputes through peaceful means. Her sincerity cannot be doubted, made as it was by a militarily much stronger party to the weaker one. Later on Nehru-Liyaqat Agreement of 8 April, 1950 provided that each country "shall ensure to the minorities throughout its territory complete equality of citizenship, irrespective of religion, a full sense of security in respect of life, culture, property and personal honour, freedom of movement within each country and freedom of occupation, speech and worship, subject to law and morality. Members of minorities shall have equal opportunity with members of the majority community to participate in the public life of their country, to hold political and other office, and to serve in their country's civil and armed forces."[3] On her part India had made appropriate provisions in her constitution. But Pakistan did not abide by its promise, thereby worsening minority conditions in both the countries. The Indus Water Treaty of 19 September 1960 is the supreme example of India's generous attitude towards Pakistan. By this treaty India not only agreed for equitable distribution of waters of the Indus basin between the two countries, but also agreed to supply water from her headworks to Pakistan until Pakistan made alternate arrangements under the treaty. She also agreed to raise the proportion of water to be supplied to Pakistan from earlier 60 per cent to 80 per cent. She also agreed to give Pakistan the aid of £62,060,000 to enable it to erect necessary structures in its territory for water utilization, while India agreed to take a loan from the World Bank to erect similar structures on her side. Since waters flow from Indian side into Pakistan, India could have withheld or stopped the supply and thereby destroyed Pakistani economy in her infancy, had India really not reconciled in the creation of Pakistan and desired coexistence with it. This treaty has stood the taste of time and India never attempted to violate it even during the periods of Indo-Pakistani wars. The Tashkent declaration of 1966 and the Simla Agreement of 1972 were the other examples of generosity shown by India towards Pakistan. By both these agreements India returned to Pakistan its territories conquered by India in the wars of 1965 and 1971 respectively without getting anything concrete in return. While India's generosity could be attributed, to some extent atleast, to the Soviet pressure, in the former case, there was no pressure on India in the latter case where India's victory over Pakistan was overwhelmingly convincing. Critics of India's generosity accused India of having lost at the negotiating table what she had gained on the battlefield. They saw India's diplomacy as the diplomacy of anti-climax, according to which Indian diplomacy gained in the initial period but lost everything in the end. The disaffection of Bangladesh and Sri Lanka with India after the latter's military support to them, for winning independence in the former case and meeting the terrorist challenge in the latter, were the other examples of India's diplomacy of anti-climax. With regard to the Simla agreement, M. J. Akbar, a prominent Muslim journalist-cum-academician and one who shared congress party secular ideology had come down very heavily on this style of Indian diplomacy. During a high level discussion about the Simla Agreement on the Indian TV on 1 July, 1992, he emphatically stated that India should have demanded the Pakistan-occupied Azad Kashmir territory, which legally belonged to India, while agreeing to return 5,000 sq. miles of Pakistani territory conquered in the war and that she should have insisted on the return of Biharis from Bangladesh to Pakistan while agreeing to repatriate 93,000 Pakistani war prisoners. He also asserted that the Kashmir question should have been explicitly settled, once for all, by the Simla Agreement. Thus by failing to do so India settled nothing with Pakistan and invited greater trouble in the subsequent period. The same attitude was again seen in 2002, when terrorist attacked the Parliament House in Delhi. This was the best opportunity for India to attack Pakistan for its alleged support to terrorists and settle all the outstanding issues permanently. But Indian leaders succumbed to international pressure and lost a golden opportunity to teach Pakistan a lesson. This, however, should not be interpreted as cowardice. Actually Indian stand was to avoid any conflict that might escalate into a major war, which might ultimately adversely affect not only India and Pakistan, but the entire South Asian region and the SAARC itself.

The aforesaid instances are mentioned here to uphold India's role, which is lost sight of while assailing India of hegemonistic designs. It is true that India's role has not been to the liking of her neighbours in many cases. The problem of trade and transit with Nepal and Bhutan because of their land-locked nature, India's opposition to make South Asia and the Indian Ocean a Zone of Peace according to Nepal's proposal, her controversies with Bangladesh regarding river waters and border problems, Sri Lanka's allegation of support to LTTE terrorists from Indian land and her displeasure at India's opposition to take any military aid from foreign countries or to allow them military bases on the Sri Lankan soil and, last but not the least, Pakistan's criticism of India for her opposition to make South Asia a nuclear free zone, are some of the instances that give rise to the fear of India's hegemonistic designs. While India cannot be completely absolved of some responsibility of causing this fear, it should be noted that a number of factors, and not India's behaviour alone, are responsible for that. These factors are as follows.

First, the fear is inherent in the situation itself. The overwhelming size, population, economic strength and military strength of India rouse apprehensions in smaller countries. Discussing the role of Germany in the European Community a German scholar says, "more than ever before we are now experiencing that a country the size of Germany in Europe - or also the USA in America, India in South Asia or Nigeria in Africa - is not loved by any of its neighbours."[4] Furthermore, India has the misfortune of having common borders with almost all the other SAARC countries, while the other countries are mostly free from this potent cause of conflict in mutual relations. India's regionalism is, therefore, essentially bilateralism. As is often said, the only constant in foreign policy is geography and unless neighbouring countries learn to live with it, it is bound to have adverse effect on their relations.

Secondly, the fear is also the hangover of the past. India is seen to follow the British imperialist policy in the region. The present-day conflicts are also the legacy of the divisive policies of the British colonialism.

Thirdly, initial Indian diplomatic inexperience coupled with adopting a moralistic attitude and pride in her greatness also contributed to the creation of a dominating image of India.

Fourthly, the other powers often misunderstood India's intentions in emphasizing the regional aspects of her security and her insistence on regional self-reliance without depending much on foreign powers. Their desire to establish their separate identities also came in the way of perceiving India's intentions in their larger context. Her geographically ordained bilateralism is viewed by others as anti-regionalism.

Fifthly, the intrusive policies of big powers also thrive on regional conflicts and differences. As pointed out by an American scholar, "For at least two decades, the United States sought to foster a balance of power between Pakistan and India in South Asia despite large differences in size. This reflected the effort to maintain Third World countries in a subsidiary position even on Third World issues by minimising the importance of the more powerful."[5] This showed that regional relations in South Asia were influenced by the policies of the extra-regional powers, some of who seek to countervail India.

Sixthly, because of her size and comparative strength India legitimately aspires to attain a global status. Her interest, therefore, goes much beyond the regional concerns, while the concerns of other SAARC countries do not generally go beyond regional connections. This global role of India affects her regional role and the other countries see in it an attempt to dominate over them.

Lastly, anti-Indian vested interests in the region also influence the smaller countries against India. These interest groups operate in the form of "Intellectuals' Think Tanks", Academicians, bureaucrats, religious groups and also some pressure groups within the political parties in both the countries as well.

Thus, India alone cannot be blamed for the fear that other countries, particularly Pakistan, feel towards her. All countries of South Asia and mainly Pakistan need to do some introspection and mould their behaviour towards one another. So far as India is concerned other SAARC countries want her to adopt a low profile. President Zia of Pakistan is reported to have suggested Indira Gandhi during an informal meeting that India should follow the example of Indonesia, which, though the largest partner in ASEAN, had deliberately played "a very docile role." Comparing India's role in SAARC with that of Indonesia in the ASEAN is, however, not fair. The kind of disparity that exists between India and the other SAARC countries does not exist between Indonesia and other ASEAN countries. India and Indonesia are comparable only in area; both are about four times larger in size than the next largest state in the region. But in other respects the comparison does not hold good. The population of India is about seven times larger than the next largest populated state in SAARC, while Indonesia's population is only about three times larger than the next populated state of ASEAN. Per capita income of major SAARC countries is almost equal, about US$ 380, though India is slightly on the lower side, while in the ASEAN the per capita income of Malaysia is about US$ 2,000 and of Singapore more than US$ 7000, while that of Indonesia is only US$ 540. The GDP of India is about six times larger than the next largest GDP state in the SAARC, while Indonesia's GDP is only about two times that of the next largest GDP state of ASEAN. India's gross industrial product is about 4/5th of the total gross industrial product of SAARC countries, while Indonesia's gross industrial product is less than ½ per cent of that of the ASEAN total.[6] Thus, Indonesia's overall position is much weaker in ASEAN than that of India in SAARC and, therefore,

Indonesia has no option but to accept a docile role. Moreover, Indonesia does not have common land border with any other ASEAN state as India has in South Asia. Indonesia has, therefore, no major cause for conflict with the other ASEAN states and hence can afford to adopt a low profile.

The suggestion that India should adopt a low profile in SAARC angers many Indian writers. They think that it is an unrealistic suggestion, harmful to India's and also the region's genuine interests. A. S. Abraham has put this aspect very forcefully. He says,. "As it stands, SAARC partakes more of illusion than reality in assuming that regional cooperation can be built on an enduring basis without reference to the realities of power.... There is basic unrealism about SAARC, which can only raise doubt about its capacity to function. It lies in pretending that the one country self-evidently preponderant in the region in every respect should not also be politically so. The assumption is that preponderance equals dominance and must, therefore, be resisted... In other words, in such a set up, Indian preponderance must be neutered to allow for supposedly genuine regional equality and fraternity.... Yet, for India, this is an invitation to political suicide.... A realistic regional grouping would not seek to ignore or circumscribe the obvious preponderance of the largest member-state, but rather, while conceding its preponderance, to deal with it in such way as to reduce the inevitable tensions and frictions that must arise in such a basically unequal relationship." Anticipating that the aforesaid view might be misunderstood as a biased statement, Mr. Abraham further clarifies, "It is necessary to emphasize that this is not an argument for India being allowed to run amuck in South Asia whenever she fears her interests are likely to be thwarted. But it is a plea for making a pendulum swing away from the other, present extreme, which is to believe that in a set up such as obtains in South Asia, the one country that naturally predominates over all others in every respect should forget this fact and that the others should also pretend it does not exist."[7]

Here Mr. Abraham rightly emphasizes that the SAARC should be based on realism and not on illusions and that distinction should be made between preponderance and domination. But he does not explain how this can be achieved. Perhaps India would do well to accept and other states would do equally well to concede India the status of being first among equals as a middle course between the two extremes of one above others and one amongst equals. This will be possible if all countries of SAARC, including India, shape their national policies as sub serving the regional interests also. They should also learn to make use of one another's strength for mutual benefit. As graphically stated by Imtiaz H. Bokhari of the Quaid-i-Azam University, Islamabad, "power in the hands of a friend is a source of strength; with a possible adversary, a source of threat."[8] Friendship, however, is not a one-way traffic. It will develop if all SAARC countries imbibe the SAARC spirit generated at the time of its inception. India's responsibility in fostering the SAARC spirit is greater in view of her preponderance in the region. For this purpose it is not necessary for India always to show 'magnanimity' or 'generosity' as demanded by many critics. It is enough if she is guided in her dealings with other SAARC countries by enlightened, and not narrow, self-interest and presents her case in a regional perspective and with due decorum. In this respect the style of the functioning of the Government of India during the Janata regime under the Prime Ministership of Morarji Desai and the Foreign Ministership of A. B. Vajpayee is worth emulating. Even in a brief period that government was successful in creating a climate of mutual understanding and friendship in South Asia. Even the present NDA government lead by Vajpayee has adopted a constructive approach.

India's position in South Asia is also compared with that of Germany in Europe. Germany is a big power in the region of highly developed countries; India is comparatively a big power among the developing and least developed countries of South Asia. Notwithstanding this basic difference there are many other points of similarity between India and Germany. Geographically, Germany is located in the heart of Europe and has common land-border with the nine of the European states just as India has common border with South Asian ones. The history of Germany under the Nazi rulers still casts its shadow on the other countries' perception of German intentions. She is the most populous country in Europe and industrially and militarily most advanced. Thus, the position of Germany in Europe resembles that of India in South Asia in many ways and both are destined to exert more influence and play a greater political role in their respective regions. For these reason both are "admired, feared and envied" in their respective regions. Like India, Germany also opposes interventions of outside powers, particularly the US, in its region. The fear of Germany puts a question mark on the unification of Europe just as fear of India creates doubts about South Asian Cooperation. Germany has, therefore, to follow a very cautious policy towards the other members of the European Economic Community. According to another German scholar Teltchik, the other countries of the ECC will get accustomed to Germany's position "if German domestic and foreign policies remain predictable."[9] This is very important. A policy, even if it is restricted to national interest, does not arouse much fear if it is predictable, and therefore, understandable. Dr. Stuth goes even further and says, "Germany's mission in Europe at the end of this century is not to dominate but to join together. There is every indication that in future Europe will not become more German but that Germany will become more European."[10] In other words, it means Germany would adopt a cooperative, rather than a domineering, style of diplomacy in the region and that her national policies would take on more and more a regional garb. India would do well to follow the same approach in South Asia. Thereby alone she will command greater and greater respect in the region and rise to her full stature. She will then become a source of strength for the region also. In fact, besides her underdeveloped condition, there is another aspect of India's economy that should give less caused for fear of India by the other SAARC countries than that of Germany in ECC. Germany's currency is too strong compared to the currencies of other countries of ECC, but Indian Rupee is weak and almost comparable in value with the other South Asian currencies. This reduces the cause of fear of India much more than that of Germany in ECC.

It appears from the above discussion that India is expected to:-

1. Adopt an approach of serving regional interest in which her enlightened self-interest would also be safe;
2. Lay primary emphasis on economic cooperation and development in the region, which will be of benefit to all countries of the region including herself;
3. Change the style of diplomacy, which would make it more cooperative and pleasant;
4. Follow predictable policies as far as possible;
5. Increase her own internal strength in all respects, but ensure that the other countries see in it no ulterior motives but enhanced support to the SAARC and its members; and
6. Adopt mutually beneficial intra-regional trade strategy.

However, a careful perusal of India's strategy or approach towards her neighbours, and particularly towards Pakistan, reveals that India has been doing the same as mentioned above. But regretfully there is no reciprocity from her neighbours and Pakistan, particularly, has always gone back on her promises.

PAKISTAN'S ROLE

Pakistan is the most important state of South Asia next to India and the future of the organization depends very crucially on the role it plays in the region. Like India, Pakistan was also initially reluctant to support the idea of SAARC and join it. It was, and continues to be, primarily afraid of India establishing its dominance in the organization. Ever since its creation Pakistan has been preoccupied with its effort to develop a separate identity from India, attain parity with it and undermine its role in the region and the world. Anti-Indianism has, therefore, become the mainstay of Pakistan's domestic and foreign policies.

Pakistan, therefore, joined SAARC ultimately with a twin purpose. It saw that for its own development regional cooperation is as much necessary for it as for the other countries of the region. Secondly, it joined the organization with the avowed purpose of preventing India from attaining any eminence in it. It, therefore, pleads for a cautious and step-by-step approach to solving regional problems. Particularly, it opposes cooperation in the core areas of trade, industry and finance as, it fears that might give advantage to India over others. All the same, it now seems to be convinced that its future lies in South Asia, and, therefore, though reluctantly, it supports its various activities.

Pakistan does not have any bilateral conflicts with the South Asian States except India and to some extent, Bangladesh. With the latter it has problems regarding settling various issues arising out of secession of Bangladesh, including the repatriation of Bihari Pakistanis. These are, however, minor issues compared to the problems it has with India. Partition of India created tremendous problems, a few of which like river water dispute, were settled amicably, others like Junagad and Pakistan does not have any bilateral conflicts with the South Asian States except India and to some extent, Bangladesh. With the latter it has problems regarding settling various issues arising out of secession of Bangladesh, including the repatriation of Bihari Pakistanis. These are, however, minor issues compared to the problems it has with India. Partition of India created tremendous problems, a few of which like river water dispute, were settled amicably, others like Junagad and refugee property, have become dormant with the passage of time. But quite a few of them have survived the vicissitudes of time and have even become increasingly critical and a few more have been added to them. Chief among the present problems are: Kashmir, the nuclear issue, the

Punjab terrorists, the Siachien Glacier, Narcotics and Smuggling. All these issues have soured Indo-Pak relations to such an extent that they have thrown a dark shadow on the future of SAARC, which has almost become a hostage to Indo-Pak relations.

Pakistan's role in the SAARC is, therefore, heavily influenced by its anti-India stance. Its policy is to use SAARC as a propaganda forum against India. It often raises bilateral and contentious issues in the SAARC meetings to embarrass India, although such issues are excluded from the purview of the SAARC Charter. It invariably supports the other SAARC states in their conflicts against India and endevours to assume their leadership in 'ganging up' against India. Pakistan believes, like many other states and writers, that unless basic bilateral, political and security issues are settled, SAARC will not have a secure foundation to build on. There is a good deal of force in this argument, but South Asian situation is unique in many respects and if it takes up such issues at the initial stage, it would be bogged down there only and might die in infancy.

The anti-India stance of Pakistan is rooted in the history of its creation. India accepted partition most reluctantly and hence, Pakistan believes India is not reconciled to its creation and wants to destroy it. It, therefore, perceives the greatest threat to its security from India. It is true that the Indian leaders were extremely upset by the partition of their country. Lord Mountabatten is reported to have told them that Pakistan, small and weak as it would be, would not be able to stand on its legs for long and, therefore, the partition would not last long. This must have won over consent of the Indian leaders to partition. The Indian leaders had also hoped that there would be some sort of a union of India and Pakistan in due course. Pakistan has thus some ground for its grievance against India. But the Indian attitude cannot be interpreted as its determination to destroy Pakistan. Had it been so, India would not have granted concessions to Pakistan after all the three Indo-Pak wars. It can be said that it was Indira Gandhi who was the first Indian Prime Minister to take a firm decision to harm Pakistan. But even in her case it was a decision to weaken Pakistan rather than completely destroy it as it was borne out by the liberal terms of the Simla Agreement.[11]

Pakistan has always been in aggressive mood since its creation, as it is evident from the fact that it masterminded attack in Kashmir soon after partition. It is on record that Jinnah was not reconciled to, what he called, a 'truncated Pakistan'. Therefore, if there was any threat to security, it was more from Pakistan to India than otherwise.

There is another and deeper reason for Pakistan's anti-India stance. Pakistan always aspired to establish parity with India. It has been, therefore, its policy to balance its strength with India by aligning militarily with the USA and to weaken India's position in every possible way. Pakistan also wants to take revenge on India for great insult it received in the Bangladesh war of 1971.

Acquisition of Kashmir has become the main factor in Pakistan's tussle against India. Since it can not win Kashmir through force it has resorted to the tactics of aiding and abetting insurgency there. For Pakistan, the validity of its separate Muslim nationalism depends on the acquisition of the Muslim majority Kashmir. For India, on the other hand, the validity of her secular nationalism equally depends on Kashmir remaining a part of India. The two points of view are, thus, totally opposed to each other and this has made the Kashmir issue almost insoluble by peaceful means.[12]

At present Pakistan seems to have adopted four-pronged strategy against India in the form of moves for weakening India through destabilisation, developing nuclear power, promoting Islamisation of India and working against India in the SAARC and other international bodies. It is nothing short of a Jehad against India unleashed by Pakistan.

Support to terrorist and secessionist activities in Punjab and Kashmir, and allegedly elsewhere in India also, is the main weapon, which Pakistan has adopted to destabilise and weaken India. Pakistan denies such an allegation and says it only gives moral and political support to the self-determination movement in Kashmir and Punjab. However, even foreign sources like USA and UK, which have normally been sympathetic to Pakistan, have confirmed Pakistan's direct support to Punjabi and Kashmiri militants and have asked Pakistan to desist from such activity. This leaves little doubt about Pakistan's direct involvement in the terrorist activities in India. This move seems to be succeeding at the moment. But its consequences would be as disastrous for Pakistan as for India. As pointed out by Lt. Gen. A. I. Akram of Pakistan himself, "Communal violence and ethnic, cultural and linguistic chauvinism are endemic to the South Asian scene. Lately, these ugly tendencies have shown an unfortunate upsurge, which is a constant source of instability in the region. The peculiarities of South Asia are such that social violence in one place acts like a volcanic eruption, and its tremors are felt far and wide."[13] The validity of this statement is borne out by the fact that simultaneously with their rise in India, terrorist and secessionist activities are on the rise in Pakistan also. It means destabilisation of India will lead to destabilisation of Pakistan also. Thus, Pakistan seems to be on a self-defeating course in its destabilisation moves. It will be pertinent to consider here the particular consequences of the terrorist and secessionist moves in Punjab and Kashmir.

Both in Punjab and in Kashmir, India's response to terrorist and secessionist challenge seems to be to contain it through military and other means and to hold on there until the terrorists get tired out. This is rather a passive strategy and does not seem to be succeeding at the moment. But India has considerable capacity to hold on and strike when appropriate opportunity arises. If India succeeds in curbing terrorism and secessionism, all Pakistan's efforts and expenditure would go waste. If, on the other hand, Pakistan succeeds in separating Punjab and/or Kashmir from India, it would still be a very costly victory for Pakistan.

For example, if Punjab succeeds in separating itself from India, its next logical step would be to demand of accession of

Pakistani Punjab to it in order to increase its viability and, for historic reasons, have the seat of Ranjit Singh's kingdom, Lahore, and the Sikh Gurudwaras in Pakistani Punjab within its territory. In Pakistan there is a lot of resistance to Punjabi dominance and it is possible that Pakistani Punjab would also desire re-union with independent Indian Punjab for linguistic and ethnic reasons. Pakistan seems to be well aware of these self-defeating consequence, and therefore, in Punjab it seems to be interested in creating only destabilization, which, as already explained, is no less harmful in its repercussions in Pakistan.

Pakistan would like Kashmir, however, to join it. Even if that happens, it won't be so for the whole state of Jammu and Kashmir. Hindu and Buddhist majority areas of Jammu and Laddakh would, in that case, opt out and stay with India and only the Kashmir valley might go to Pakistan. It would, thus, be a truncated Kashmir that Pakistan would get and it would be a heavy liability on Pakistan. As it is, India has been pouring vast amounts of funds - Rs.40,000 crores during the past 50 years, according to one estimate - to sustain Kashmir. Pakistan, with its meager resources would not be able to match India's efforts and so the Kashmiris would soon get disaffected with Pakistan, adding further to the latter's internal worries. However, Kashmir's opting for Pakistan seems to be remote possibility. It might prefer an independent status. Even in the Azad Kashmir area on the Pakistani side of the Line of Actual Control (LAC), there is a strong demand for independence. The Jammu and Kashmir Liberation Front (JKLF), which hitherto received support from Pakistan and is based in Azad Kashmir, is working for independence of Kashmir under the leadership of Amanullah Khan and Pakistan is finding it difficult to restrain him. Hence, even if Pakistan succeeds in achieving secession of Kashmir valley from India, it would lead to secession of Azad Kashmir from Pakistan also. The independent, united, Kashmir would still be an unviable state and prove to be constant headache both for India and Pakistan, situated as it would be between them and China and the former Soviet states. Pakistan's

Kashmir policy, therefore, seems to be based more on emotions than on hard realistic considerations.[14] Azad Kashmir, is working for independence of Kashmir under the leadership of Amanullah Khan and Pakistan is finding it difficult to restrain him. Hence, even if Pakistan succeeds in achieving secession of Kashmir valley from India, it would lead to secession of Azad Kashmir from Pakistan also. The independent, united, Kashmir would still be an unviable state and prove to be constant headache both for India and Pakistan, situated as it would be between them and China and the former Soviet states. Pakistan's Kashmir policy, therefore, seems to be based more on emotions than on hard realistic considerations.

In the past, two attempts were made to solve the Kashmir problem peacefully and to the satisfaction of both India and Pakistan. The UN resolution on Kashmir of April 21, 1948 and the Simla Agreement of 1972 were these efforts. Pakistan still demands the settlement of the Kashmir issue in accordance with these agreements. However, closer scrutiny reveals that Pakistan has been primarily responsible for the non-implementation of these agreements. According to the modalities worked out under the UN resolution to create conditions for holding free and fair referendum in Kashmir, Pakistan was required to pull out all its forces from the areas occupied by it as, being an aggressor, it had no *locus-standi* there. India, on her part, was also required to remove the bulk of her forces from the area under her control, but was allowed to keep minimum force there to maintain law and order which was her legal responsibility as Jammu and Kashmir had legally acceded to it, like other Indian princely states, through an instrument of accession. Pakistan failed to pull out its forces and thus fulfill the pre-condition for holding plebiscite, in spite of its agreement to do so.

With regard to the Simla Agreement, it is now confirmed that India and Pakistan recognized that Kashmir was a matter of dispute between them on an oral understanding that it would be settled peacefully by transforming the LAC into an international border. During a discussion on Simla Agreement held on Doordarshan on 1 July, 1992, Mr. S. K. Singh, former Indian Foreign Secretary, who was present at Simla at the time of the Simla Agreement, asserted that the Pakistani Prime Minister, Mr. Bhutto, gave a verbal assurance to India that the LAC in Kashmir would be made international border and that he would persuade his people to agree to it. He, however, pleaded for not reducing this understanding into writing in the agreement as that might make his task difficult in the condition of roused passions of his people in those days. Thus division of state of Jammu and Kashmir at the LAC by legalizing the status quo could have been the most satisfactory solution of the problem. But Pakistan not only went back on its word, but roused the passions of its people still further to make the solution most difficult.

But this upsurge might not last long and the secular interest, alleast the basic ones, cultivated during communist rule might again become fairly prominent there. Moreover, Islam by itself is no longer a unifying force in the national and international arena. Unification of the whole region on the plank of Islam, as desired by Pakistan, does not, therefore, seem to be a possibility. In any case Pakistan will have to contend with Iran and Turkey for supremacy in the region in which the latter will have advantage over Pakistan. Ethnically and interestwise the Central Asian states are closer to Turkey than Pakistan. For all these reasons and for all the enthusiasm Pakistan shows for the development of this region, it would soon find itself as alien in Central Asia as in West Asia. While it may still be able to develop certain advantageous relations with Central Asia, it would not be able to get completely accepted as its part. The sooner Pakistan realises this, the better.

In view of the inextricably interwoven nature of Indo-Pak interests and relations, the partition of the sub-continent now appears to have been a questionable move. The Cabinet Mission Plan which aimed at providing autonomy to Muslim majority areas without destroying the unity of the sub-continent would have been the best solution of the Hindu-Muslim problem. Even Jinnah was agreeable to it. But Nehru's indiscreet statement questioning the finality of grouping of areas destroyed the whole scheme. Even then the need for close association between the two countries was felt by responsible people on both sides of the border right from the time of the partition.[15] There was a talk of joint military command in those days. Nehru's desire for eventual Indo-Pak association is obvious from the aforesaid statement. Even Jinnah, after partition, stated in a broadcast on 19-2-1948, "We have no aggressive designs upon our neighbours. We wish to live in peace and friendship and to workout our destiny quietly in our own way and make our rightful contribution in the affairs of the world."[16] Mr. Zafrullah Khan, the most astute Foreign Minister of Pakistan in the 50s, remarked: "if they (i.e. India and Pakistan) stood together, (they) could play in world affairs an almost decisive role." As time passed, more and more leaders of Pakistan, including Z. A. Bhutto, Ms. Bhutto, Khan Wali Khan and G. M. Sayyed of the 'Jiye-Sindh movement', have expressed themselves in favour of ending the era of conflict between India and Pakistan and forging some sort of association between the two for mutual benefit. Former Chief Minister of West Punjab, Hanif Ramay, who was very close to Mr. Z. A. Bhutto, in an interview to Urdu Daily 'Jung' had said that Mr. Bhutto had thought of a confederation of India and Pakistan in which he would be the President and Mrs. Indira Gandhi the Prime Minister. This had been corroborated by another associate of Mr. Bhutto, Mr. Hamid Mohammed, also.[17] The Sindhi Leader of Pakistan, G. M. Sayyed, who had moved the Pakistan Resolution in the Sindh Legislative Assembly soon became disillusioned with the partition and favoured a confederation of India and Pakistan.[18] Ms. Benazir Bhutto has written in her book, 'Pakistan : The Gathering Storm' about Indo-Pak relations, that "All sections of patriotic opinion (in Pakistan) are now convinced that these relations need to be improved. Indeed, we must work for a rapprochement."[19] There is no dearth of intellectuals and statesmen from India, who see the desirability of Indo-Pak rapprochement. The former Prime Minister of India, Mr. P. V. Narsimha Rao, for example, in his address as India's External Affairs Minister to the Pakistan Institute of International Affairs in Karachi, on 11 June, 1981, candidly analyzed the whole gamut of Indo-Pak relations and, in the end remarked, "In conclusion, I would venture a few words about my vision for the future of Indo-Pakistan relations.......... I am trying to look beyond the stage of normalization and aim at positive friendship based on active cooperation born of genuine mutual trust. I think we have to undertake a deliberate and conscious transformation of our respective psyches."[20]

It is, therefore, high time that the rulers of Pakistan changed their stance towards India. The future of both the countries and of the whole region of South Asia depends critically on it. From this point of view, it is not India but Pakistan that is central to the survival and development of SAARC.

Since emotions come in the way of pragmatic assessment by Pakistan of the internal as well as the regional situation, the intellectuals of Pakistan can play a crucial role in bringing about rational changes in the Pakistan policies. The development of non-official level of discussions between the intellectuals of India and Pakistan is welcome development in this respect. The first three-days dialogue between Indo-Pak intellectuals was held in October, 1991 in India and it was followed by second round in Pakistan in January, 1992. This form of public diplomacy, also called Track-III Diplomacy, will improve each other's perceptions and clear misunderstandings and create a better climate for improving Indo-Pak ties. In the interest of SAARC also this is the most constructive development in Indo-Pak relations. Ever since its creation, Pakistan has been obsessed with the question of attaining parity with India. This was almost an unattainable objective, considering vast disparities of almost every type between the two countries. However, by developing its nuclear capability Pakistan has now achieved parity of the highest type, from security point of view, with India. A major war between the two countries is now unthinkable. Pakistan should, therefore, now feel assured of its security against India. This should, therefore, lay at rest all its fears about perceived threats from India. It should now be able to calmly consider how to put its relations with India on a positive base of mutual benefit and good neighbourly relations. More Muslims live in India than in Pakistan, and if Pakistan has any consideration for their peaceful living and well-being, it should regard India as '*Dar-ul-Aman*' (House of Friendship) and not a '*Dar-ul-Islam*' (House of War). That is the only alternative to mutual destruction. If that happens - and that seems to be the only pragmatic possibility - the deterrent nuclear development would prove to be a boon in disguise.[21]

SAARC has adopted a very cautious approach right from its birth. No discussion on bilateral & controvertial issues, Primacy given to issues of common concern and Unanimity in decision-making are the three guiding functional principles adopted by SAARC. The last one acts like a veto power, which means when even a single country has some different view point, decisions can not be taken until all agree. This is strength as well as weakness of SAARC. Strength because once there is unanimity on an issue decision is quick and its implementation is also fast & with full sincerity. Weakness because the veto power can be used by any state to stall good, progressive decisions which are genuinely in the region's interest. For example;

a. India opposed Bangladesh proposal on exploitation of water resources between herself, Nepal & India. India opposed it on the ground that it was more of a bilateral issue between India & Bangladesh. But later the scope of the issue was widened and it was taken up as an area of ecological imbalance and disaster management.

b. India had reservation about the Convention on Suppression of Terrorism. Sri Lanka also harboured different approach on this issue. The Convention is drafted on the lines of latest International Conventions, but suffers from inherent defects. There is no clear definition of Terrorism and Terrorist. All the actions depend on the sweet-will of the concerned state.

c. Pakistan has been consistently opposing cooperation in the core areas of economy and trade. It feared that its domestic and international interests would be jeopardized by that. But gradually, she was convinced about the importance of economic cooperation and trade relations and SAARC signed a very important agreement like SAPTA.

d. The postponement of 11th SAARC Summit at Kathmandu because of sudden military coup in Pakistan and India's refusal to recognize it and the latest deferment of 12th SAARC Summit to be held in Islamabad, due to stubborn stands taken by India and Pakistan, are the latest glaring examples of fragile nature of SAARC and its dependence on Indo-Pak relations.

e. Atomic Explbsions carried out by both in May 1998 changed the strategic positions of both and with the inclusion in the exclusive "Nuclear Club" both are now in a position to negotiate on equal terms.

The above examples indicate that all is not well within SAARC and Indo-Pak relations pose a great threat to the working of SAARC. It is not so. India and Pakistan have cooperated constructively and shown greater magnanimity in resolving many regional as well as bilateral issues. The SAARC Charter prohibits discussion on political and contentious issues. But some of the decisions of SAARC have crossed that barrier boldly. Most important decision in this regard has been the Convention on Narcotic Drugs and Psychotropic Substances which was ratified by all the SAARC countries and it came into force in September, 1993. Similarly, SAARC VISA Exemption Scheme became operational in March, 1992. SAARC also undertook a study on combatting the crime of trafficking in women and children for prostitution. SAARC also concentrated on constructive cooperation in the fields of women development, child welfare and protection of girlchild. The Dhaka Resolution on Women was accepted as an official SAARC position to be presented at the forthcoming 4th World Conference on Women. 2001-10 A.D. has been declared as the 'SAARC Decade of the

Rights of the Child.' Similarly 3rd Ministerial Conference on Children of South Asia held in 1996 called for elimination of childlabour by 2010 A.D. Tourism is another area which SAARC decided to give boost to. First SAARC Film Festival was held in Colombo in 1998. Festival of SAARC countries was also held at New Delhi in 1992. The scheme of SAARC Youth Awards was started in 1997. SAARC also sponsored two important independent studies - (a) Causes and consequences of natural disasters and preservation of the environment; and (b) Green House effect and its impact on the region. SAARC also introduced some administrative changes. The number of technical Committees was brought down to 11 from 13 by merging Postal Services with Communication and Health with Population and Child Welfare to promote cohesiveness in SAARC activities. Similarly, the term of SAARC Secretary-General has been increased to 3 years from 2 in 1997. This is intended to give him more time to devote himself to more constructive contribution to SAARC.Steps were also taken to forge closer practical cooperation with the EU and the ASEAN in the meeting of the SAARC Council of Ministers' held at New York in 1999. SAARC also prepared a collective agenda of concerns for presentation at WTO meeting in Seattle in 2000.[22]Steps were also taken to forge closer practical cooperation with the EU and the ASEAN in the meeting, referred to earlier, of the SAARC Council of Ministers' held at New York in 1999.(8) SAARC also prepared a collective agenda of concerns for presentation at WTO meeting in Seattle in 2000.

The above decisions show that SAARC is progressing steadily in social and non-controvertial fields. These activities are not hampered by the political uncertainties and conflicts.

However, the biggest challenge that has come before SAARC has been the atomic explosions of India and Pakistan in May, 1998. But unilateral moratorium on further explosions and declaration of 'no-first-use' policy by India eased tension considerably. Furthermore, on bilateral level launching of Delhi-Lahore bus in February, 1999 proved to be soothing effect on Indo-Pak relations.

However, it was short-lived when Pak-sponsored terrorists and Afghan guerillas clandestinely occupied Indian positions on J & K border in Kargil area in May, 1999 and a bloody armed conflict ensued. India occupied all her positions at tremendous cost to both the countries. It created turmoil in Pakistan. But, it is significant to note, all these tensions did not stop diplomatic exchanges and Delhi-Lahore bus and train services between India and Pakistan and usual trade also continued unaffected.

There was military coup in Pakistan in October, 1999 led by Gen. Musharraf, the very next day when a democratically elected government led by Shri. Atal Bihari Vajpayee took over in India. India refused to do business with the military ruler and instead demanded return of democracy in Pakistan. The scheduled SAARC Summit in Kathmandu was also postponed as India declined to participate in it in the changed atmosphere and thereby give recognition to the new military ruler of Pakistan. India also successfully supported move to expel Pakistan from NAM and the Commonwealth.

These developments have put a break on the progress of SAARC. This is by far the greatest crisis the SAARC is facing today. It has once again proved that SAARC is hostage to Indo-Pak relations. The reality at present is that the two most powerful actors in SAARC, India and Pakistan, are nuclear powers. It is a deterrent for them. They have reached a stage where even a small skirmish can trigger off a major war. This is not in their advantage. Pakistan, emboldened by its nuclear capability and with ever-aggressive military ruler, is now bent upon solving the Kashmir issue by encouraging cross-border clashes and attacks on civilians as well as military establishments in J & K. India has realized this danger and adopted a pro-active strategy to eliminate Pak-sponsored terrorism in J & K. She is producing indigenous weapons and rockets, modernising her forces and increasing her defence budget for 2000-01. Some skeptics regard Indo-Pak conflict as a permanent feature of South Asia and feel that there will be constant tension between

India and Pakistan leading to increase in defense expenditure. However, there is some hope which answers the doubts raised by the skeptics. First, Pakistan is now mostly isolated in the world. Mis-adventure in Kargil has proved Pakistan's involvement beyond doubt. US and other countries have stopped aid to Pakistan, which has shaken the Pak economy. Therefore, Pakistan can not dare to stretch its anti-Indianism and proxy war beyond a limit. Some day, it will have to come to negotiating table. In fact, the military ruler of Pakistan is very eager to enter into negotiations with India. But India refuses to oblige him unless Pak support to trans-border terrorism is stopped. Secondly, there is tremendous pressure on Pakistan to return to democracy. Particularly, the hitherto closest ally of Pakistan, the US, wants Pakistan to have a democratically elected government. Pakistan cannot afford to invite wrath of USA. These international pressures and internal compulsions will force Pakistan to follow the path of wisdom.

India's image has received a positive boost after the terrorist attack on WTC in USA mainly because India's mature and consistent stand on the issue of terrorism. Indian view is global and international community has appreciated it after September 11. Other reasons behind this boosting up of India's image are: her tactful handling of the post Pokhran-II situation; her befitting though measured response to Kargil intrusion; her patience after attack on Indian Parliament and firm stand on many other issues in spite of sanctions and pressures. It has also been proved beyond doubt that Indian economy is still sound enough to absorb shocks and is an attraction for foreign investors and marketeers.

India and Pakistan are now both virtual nuclear powers. This has made the South Asian region, according to US view, the greatest flashpoint of world conflict. However, as pointed out in the book, it would be more reasonable to say that India and Pakistan have now entered a cold war stage between them similar to the one that existed between the US and the Soviet Union after the 2nd World War. In this situation all kinds of conflicts, including local wars like the Kargil one, might arise between the two but they would not escalate into a full-fledged nuclear war. The leaders of the two countries will not take such a suicidal step and the people of the two countries will not favour it.

This is not to deny the adverse effects of the Indo-Pak crisis on SAARC. Many of its activities have slowed down. But this seems to be a temporary phase. For, the activities already decided upon are proceeding smoothly including efforts to turn SAPTA into SAFTA. The former SAARC Secretary-General, Nihal Rodrigo, toured all the SAARC countries, including India and Pakistan, between 28 March and 30 May, 2000, to assess their outlook on SAARC and to discuss continuing SAARC activities and future programmes. He observed that there is strong resolve at the highest levels to carry out SAARC activities with fullest commitment to the SAARC spirit.[23] This is very encouraging observation. There are many incidents which could have affected the SAARC spirit. However, these actually reflect the resolve and commitment of the leaders of India and Pakistan to carry out the agenda of regional cooperation and do not allow these strained relations to come in the way of SAARC. For example:-

a. Pakistan showed great farsight in proposing addition of new areas in the SAARC activities like Education and Women. Similarly it was Pakistan who proposed to initiate cooperation in the field of HRD. All these proposals were readily agreed by all others.

b. There has been some bright side also. SAARC has helped to diffuse tension between India & Pakistan. Most significant example of this was the SAARC Summit held at Islamabad in 1988. This was a Summit which was actually to be held in Colombo, but Sri Lanka was not ready to host it because of Tamil Issue. So Pakistan volunteered to hold it. The 1988 SAARC Summit is unique in many ways. India was represented by Rajiv Gandhi, Indian Prime Minister who visited Pak after 25 years. He was son of Indira Gandhi, who was responsible for Pak's humiliating defeat in 1971. Pakistan's Prime Minister was Benazir Bhutto, daughter of Z. A. Bhutto, the then Prime Minister of Pakistan who had to face defeat in 1971. The family lineage is significant here. In spite of this background the SAARC Summit was held in the most cordial atmosphere.

c. Second significant fact is that there was Indo-Pak Bilateral Summit within the SAARC Summit. Three important agreements were signed – (a) Non-attack on each others' N-establishments and exchange of information about military movements, (b) Avoidance of double-taxation, (c) Cultural cooperation. This is very significant move. It shows the resolve of the two countries to move forward. Besides the burden of the past was not evident between the leaders of India and Pakistan.

d. India under the leadership of PM Atal Bihari Vajpayee took the initiative of starting a Bus service from New Delhi to Lahore. He even traveled in the inaugural bus journey and was received with great enthusiasm in Pakistan. This shows that noble ways with good intentions always yield good results. India has always tried to establish normal relations with Pakistan.

e. The above noble gesture from India, however, was rewarded with sudden infiltration of army by Pakistan in the strategically sensitive positions on J & K border like Kargil. India had to take strong military action to recapture her land and military bases. This was almost like a war for India, though legally it was not termed so. This incident gave a set back to the good will created by the Bus Service.

f. From the days of Kargil till today there is continuous tension in Indo-Pak relations. In spite of this fact the normal relations in non-political fields between the two countries continued, like the Bus service, train service, pilgrimages etc. India had to take a stubborn stand and drastic step of recalling our High Commissioner from Pak for a brief period and she is justified in doing so in the prevailing situation. India had to express its anger, anguish.

g. The relations further worsened when there was military coup in Pakistan, overthrowing the democratically elected govt. of Nawaz Sharif. India refused to recognize this change of regime; first, because a democratically elected govt. was overthrown and second, because the reins in Pak were taken over by General Parwez Musharraf, Army chief of Pakistan who was regarded as the main architect and brain behind the Kargil adventure and thus was a Villain for India. India has always supported democratic Pakistan and a democratically elected govt. in Pakistan. Experience has proved that relations between the two have been cordial whenever there was an elected govt. in Islamabad. Relations nose-dived whenever there was a military regime in Pak. Exactly the same thing happened when Musharraf took over the reigns in Pak.

h. Even in this odd situation India invited Musharraf for talks at Agra. Musharraf took a stubborn position that Kashmir is the central issue and the rest are secondary issues between India & Pakistan. India did not agree to this and demanded that Pakistan must first stop cross-border terrorism and close down all the training camps in its territory. India was ready to discuss all the issues on this pre-condition. Agra Summit thus ended without any conclusion as both the sides were not ready to dilute their positions. After this event, India and Pak continued to use various international fora to ventilate their views.

i. There was terrorist attack on the Indian Parliament in December, 2001, which was considered to be an attack on Indian democracy itself. It was the most serious attempt to disturb Indian polity. Pakistan's involvement was proved beyond doubt. India made all the preparations to take revenge and alerted its troops on the border. But India showed great restraint and did not allow the tension to escalate into a war.

j. Another serious period in Indo-Pak relations occurred when Indian diplomats in Islamabad were tortured by Pak authorities and subsequently were asked to leave the country. India also retaliated by expelling some senior diplomats from Pak High Commission in Delhi. Later even the High Commissioners were taken back. It was the greatest diplomatic set back in Indo-Pak relations. But fortunately this did not become a cause for any armed conflict.

Even in this situation, normal relations in other areas continued at the governmental level, also called Track-II Diplomacy. In 2002, India's I&B minister was in Islamabad to participate in a ministerial level meeting of SAARC. Pakistan on that occasion organized an exhibition of ruins and excavations of Harrappan civilization. Meetings of various technical committees, secretary-level committees and negotiations at the ministerial level are going on without interruption under the SAARC. SAARC has adopted a most effective and novel way of cooperation, i.e: People-to-people cooperation, i.e: Track III diplomacy. This is being carried out in the fields of Tourism, Cultural Exchanges, Educational exchanges, TV-radio programmes etc. SAARC has provided this opportunity for India and Pakistan to maintain a minimum level of relations, at least at the official/secretarial and peoples' level, if not at the highest political level. This kind of cooperation is very crucial for countries like India and Pakistan, who were partitioned not only geographically, but were separated socially, culturally, religiously and family-wise also. There is still present a bond of brotherhood & love among the common masses of both the countries. This has been testified by number of academicians, journalists, students, artists and govt. officials who frequently visit each other across the border. This indicates that somewhere in the hearts of hearts there is a feeling of cooperation and love among the people of India and Pakistan. This feeling is kept alive by the SAARC. Because of SAARC there is some level of communication between the two countries. SAARC Summits provide an indirect opportunity for the leaders to come together informally and discuss bilateral issues. Most successful example of Islamabad Summit is sited above. An example of contrary nature is of Kathmandu Summit of 2002, where the two leaders did not go beyond shaking hands and exchange of pleasantries. This, however, does not undermine the importance of the SAARC as a forum to bring the two countries together.

The scheduled SAARC Summit to be held at Islamabad by the end of 2002 has been postponed obviously because of the present stand off between India and Pakistan. There are other factors responsible for this like the situation in the Gulf, which has caught the attention of the entire world.

To sum up, it is true that the future of SAARC hangs in balance as never before. It has been proved again that SAARC is hostage to Indo-Pak relations. But it will be again SAARC that will help the two countries to resume their normal relations. One major obstacle is the undemocratic rule in Pak. The Musharraf regime is surviving on American Oxygen presently, because America is hoping that Musharraf will provide them support in their anti-Laden operations. That is America's compulsion and Musharraf is shrewd enough to realize that and use it for his own survival. Yet, there is some hope that SAARC will progress even in odd situations. The reasons for this hope is :- (a) In spite of Kargil and military takeover in Pakistan the old train service and the newly introduced bus service between New Delhi and Lahore continue to operate; (b) Trade and diplomatic relations continue as before; (c) Track-II diplomacy between the two countries has been proceeding quietly at Colombo with Sri Lanka as host; (d) There is tremendous international pressure on Pakistan to stop assistance to terrorists in Kashmir and to return to democracy; and (e) Last but not the least, people-to-people contacts between the two countries at all levels, including recent exchange of visits by women's delegations of the two countries, are going on without hindrance. These facts indicate that the SAARC will survive in the present strained situation and also someday provide a platform for India and Pakistan to come together. These hopes will be buried only if the military rulers of Pakistan attempt a military solution of the Kashmir problem, which in spite of Pakistani threats seems most unlikely in view of its nuclear consequences. So presently all have to wait and watch. The course in South Asia depends on the situation in the Gulf as well as South-East Asia. But the fact remains that it will be SAARC that will provide a forum for India and Pakistan to re-establish their normal relations. Leaders of both the countries have fully understood the importance of SAARC and realized that in the post-atomic explosion scenario they can survive jointly or perish separately. They also know that success of SAARC depends on their mutual relations. So they will attempt to utilize SAARC to advance their respective national interests as a pressure tactic, but will not stretch it too far to break the Organization itself.

REFERENCES:

1. Quoted by Kashikar, S. G. in "*Antararashtriya Sambandh*", (1983), Maharashtra Universities Textbook Production Board, Nagpur; p.199.
2. "A New Impetus and Fresh Direction"; External Publicity Division, Ministry of External Affairs, Government of India, New Delhi, 1986.
3. Mahmood, M.: "Regional Integration in South Asia – Perspectives and Prospects"; S. Chand & Co., Delhi, 1987; p.66.
4. Stuth, Reinhard : "Germany's New Role in Changing Europe"; Aussen Politik, Vol.43, No.1, 1st Quarter, 1992; German Foreign Affairs Review, Humburg; p.23.
5. Quoted by Baral, Lok Raj : "SARC, But No SHARK" in Pacific Affairs, Vol. 58, No.3; Fall-1985, p.417.

6. Pradhan, Bishwa; "SAARC and Its Future", Kathmandu, 1988.
7. Abraham, A. S. : "SAARC's Basic Unrealism"; The Times of India, Mumbai, 27-06-1987.
8. Bokhari, Imtiaz H.: South Asian Regional Cooperation"; Asian Survey, Vol. XXV, No.3, March-1985, p.380.
9. Teltchik, Horst : "Germany's New Role in the New Order"; The German Tribune, Humburg, 14-02-1992.
10. Stuth, Reinhard; op.cit., p.32.
11. Nagarkar, V. V. : "Genesis of Pakistan"; Allied Publishers, Mumbai, 1975, Pp.18-75.
12. ibid.;
13. Akram, A. I. : "Security and Stability in South Asia" in Cohen, Stephen Philip (ed.), "Security of South Asia – American and Asian Perspective"; Vistaar, Delhi, 1987, Pp.176-178.
14. Kashikar, M. S.; "SAARC: Its Genesis, Development and Prospect", Himalaya Publishing House, Mumbai, 2000, Pp.192-3.
15. Azad, Abul Kalam : "India Wins Freedom"; Orient Longman, Hyderabad, 1988, p.170.
16. "Quid-e-Azam Mohammad Ali Jinnah : Speeches as Governor General of Pakistan (1947-48)"; Government of Pakistan Publication, Karachi, p.59.
17. The Nagpur Times, Nagpur; 2-12-1985.
18. The Nagpur Times, Nagpur; 18-10-1990.
19. Bhutto, Benazir : "Pakistan – The Gathering Storm"; Vikas Publishing House, New Delhi, 1983, p.66.
20. *India Quarterly*, (Text of the Speech); ICWA, Delhi, Vol.37, No.3, September-1987, p.413.
21. Kashikar, M.S.; op.cit.; p.203.
22. *SAARC NEWS*; newsletter of the SAARC Secretariat, Kathmandu, various issues.
23. ibid.

9

Proxy War : In The Shadow of Indo-Pak Relations

Ram Dev Bharadwaj

Terrorism is a major factor for destabilizing any country in the world, however it is a global problem for the contemporary world. It has affected both the developing as well as the developed countries.. At present, India is facing its most significant security problems as a result of insurgency and terrorist activities in sensitive Jammu and Kashmir state. This is generally due to peculiar geography and demography of the state. Pakistan has intensified its proxy war in J&K by pushing terrorists, including the latest brand of suicide bombers, to disrupt the fragile peace in the state. The Kashmir conflict has occupied the center stage of South Asia politics and diplomacy, since independence. The then General Shankar Roy Chaudhary gave a frank view as a solder about the proxy war in Kashmir by saying that, "What is happening in Kashmir is an undeclared war by Pakistan. They are not only backing the different insurgent outfits working against India but also sending mercenaries who cross the border and directly fight with our force".[1]

PROXY WAR AND TERRORISM

Pakistan is today one of the main centers of Islamic

fundamentalism, drug trafficking, illicit trade in small arms and international terrorism. She has never failed to exploit anti-Indian sentiments with Kashmir as the centerpiece. The power structure in Pakistan survives on hate India campaign. The mullahs, the army, the bureaucracy and the feudal lords exercise the real power in Pakistan. They have their differences but the feudal lords exercise real power in Pakistan. Power and privileges are concentrated in their hands . However, their hostility towards is implacable. It is obvious that Pakistan is banking on the combination of an attack across the LoC with large-scale violence in the valley to capture Jammu and Kashmir. There is also information that there are nearly thousand mercenaries and intruders functioning in different parts of the valley. Pakistan has learnt the lesson of 1947-48, 1965 and 1971 and they are now engaged in a structured, long-term politico-military operation to grab Kashmir.

The Palestine Liberation Organization (PLO) was the first to introduce airline hijacking as an international weapon to terrorize its opponents. The European Radical Faction was another group, which carried out increasingly indiscriminate bombing, kidnapping and assassinations throughout the targeted countries. These terrorist groups, seemingly independent of each other soon proliferated throughout Europe, Japan, North and South America, and the Islamic Middle East. In Asian Countries, India is worse affected country in this context. There is a large number of terrorist organizations functioning in Jammu and Kashmir by direct and indirect supervision of Inter Service Intelligence (ISI), Jammu and Kashmir Liberation Front (JKLF), *Harkat-ul-Ansar* (HuA) now *Harkat-ul- Mujahideen* (HuM), *Lashkar-e-Toiba* (LeT), *Hizab-ul-Mujahideen*, (HuM),*Al-Badar*,*Al-Faran*,*Al-jehad*,*Al-Baraz*,*Allah-tiger*,*Zia-Tigar*,*Al-umer-Mujahideen*, *Dukhataram-e-Millat* (DeM), *Jamait-ul-Mujahideen* (JuM),*Jaish-e-Muhammad* (JeM),*Tehreek-e-Mujahideen* (TeM) are the main militant groups at present functioning in Jammu and Kashmir. Saudi billionaire Osama-Bin-Laden is also involved with Pakistan Government through *Harkat-ul-Ansar* and *Al-badar*. These terrorist groups have been provided sophisticated communication gadgets and weapons by Pakistan in the name of Islamic '*jehad*', and trained them in various safe places in Pakistan, PoK and Afghanistan.

GENESIS OF 'OPERATION TOPAC' AND PROXY WAR 1998

Pakistan understands that, Kashmir cannot be captured from India by direct or indirect conflict. So, late General Zia-ul-Haq conceived operation 'Topac' in 1988 with the aim of annexing Kashmir through a 'low cost' and 'no cost' action suited to Pakistan's geo-political, diplomatic and military interests.[2] The operation 'Topac' was to be executed through a well planned and meticulously executed three phases 'operation by the ISI. The phase I was to initiate low-level insurgency, sub verse police, financial and communication institutions, organize and train submarine element in Kashmir sabotage communication and create chaos in Jammu and Kashmir and to establish control over areas not covered by the Indian Army'.[3]

The phase II was the direct pressure along the LoC, infiltrate Afghan Mujahideens and indirect special force to attack strategic targets.[4] Attack and destroy base depots and headquarters located in Srinagar, Pattan, Kupwara, Baramulla, Bandipur etc, by covert action at the given time. A special force from Azad Kashmir along with hard core militant will be prepared to attack and destroy Kargil-Leh Highway, Radio station, Doordarshan Kendra, airfield and block Banihal Tunnel.

The phase III and last was to intensify 'jehad' to liberate Kashmir,[5] to destroy India's conventional strength, to internationalize J & K issue, denounce Indian Army over Human Rights violation and paint India as an anti-Muslim, Hindu fundamentalist country with hegemonic ambition.

MILITANCY, PROXY WAR AND KARGIL STAND-OFF

The period of militancy in the Kashmir called can be broadly classified into five parts :-

(a) The period of militancy – up to 1990

(b) The proxy war – up to 1998

(c) The Kargil conflict – 1999

(d) Operation Vijay and post Kargil situation

(e) Post Kargil situation

(a) The period of militancy – up to 1990

Despite the tight vigil on the LoC between two countries by the Indian security forces, a large number of mercenaries managed to infiltrate into the valley. During 1988-89, there were at least forty-four terrorist organisations operating in the valley and important amongst them were the JKLF, the Hizab-ul-Mujahideen, the Student Liberation Front, the People League, the Operation Balakote, the Kashmir Liberation Tiger, the Zia Tiger and the Al- Khomeni. That means the phase I operation 'Topac' was warning bell in Kashmir. Major incidents in J&K during the period were as under:-

(a) In February 1984, Ravindra Mhatra, an Indian diplomat posted at Birmingham was kidnapped by JKLF and murdered in UK.[6]

(b) Pakistan Chief Executive Gen. Zia's death in August 1988 in an air crash was a set back but not serious enough to stall the phase I Operation 'Topac'.

(c) In 1989, an eleven party alliance was formed in 'Azad Kashmir' to help the freedom struggle in Kashmir and the Pak People's Party (PPP) also started playing the Kashmir card. The period was marked by agitation's, demonstrations, bomb blasts and selected targeting of Kashmiri Pandit to give it communal overtones.[7]

(d) On December 8. 1989, Dr Rubiyya Sayeed, daughter of the

Home Minister in the National Front Government at the centre, Mufti mohammad Sayeed, was kidnapped by the Yasin Malik, one of the infamous terrorist and the president of JKLF. She was released in exchange of five hard core JKLF terrorist including Abdul Hamid Sheikh, Javed Zarar and Sher Khan.[8]

(e) General strike was observed in Pakistan on February 5, 1990 to express solidarity with the Kashmir and all political parties displayed the placards " Kashmir will be in Pakistan". [9]

(f) The killing of Mirza Maulana Mohammad Farooq, the Chairman of Awami Action Committee along with 57 persons on the funeral procession on March 24, 1990.

(b) 'The Proxy War upto 1998

The period was marked by escalation strikes against selected targets. It had started in the summer month of 1990. As a result, the valley and the 20-km belt of Rajouri and Poonch areas were declared disturbed on July 5, 1990. The year 1991-92 saw escalation on military activities and intensification of counter-insurgency operation by security forces in Kupwara, Doda and Uri sector.[10] Allegation of mass rape at Kunar, Poshpora in Kupwara in Feb 1991 and other incidents were exploited by militants to put pressure on the government. Ekta Yatra of Murli Manohar Joshi of BJP and Ammanullah Khan of JKLF efforts to organize a people march, which was prevented by the Pakistan government, were other events of significance. According to the Task Force, the ISI of Pakistan provided the terrorists and other militants with new weapons. During the summer 1993, they were also provided with powerful long range missiles called 'Chemical' by the Sikhs, who had learned about them while undergoing training in Pakistan.

But the situation turned significant during the summer of 1993 with the appointment of General K.V. Krishna Rao as the new Governor of the state. He outlined a somewhat more cohesive policy in the field of militancy, revamping the administration, revival of political activity and dealing with alienation of the people. As a result, the years 1993 -1994 saw huge losses of lives of terrorists of Pakistan. Though there was increase in criminal activities yet people gradually turned away from the militants. However, on June 20, 1994, the Islamic terrorists assassinated the Kashmiri scholar Quzi Nissar Ahmad who was kidnapped a night before and was pressured to endorse the anti-Indian *jehad*. He refused and was killed by the terrorists.

The year 1995 and the period after this was marked a high rate drop outs of Kashmiri militants due to heavy casualties. 1995 and the period after this was marked by a pronounced change in the configuration and orientation of insurgency. The militancy picture was not completed without taking into account of events of Hazratball in Oct 1993 and the Charer-e-Sharif incident in Mar 1995. [11] While the first was a success but the second can be termed as a failure.

The year 1996-97 were marked by pro-active initiatives in the political field by holding election to the J&K assembly and installation of an elected government in November 1996. Along with the above political process, the situation of the state was marked by two major trends. Firstly, that the proxy war had passed into the hands of the foreign mercenaries operating under the direct control of ISI and secondly, it had taken root in the areas of Poonch, Rajouri, Doda and Pirpanjal Range and there were attacks on isolated Hindu village Doda in the district of Udhampur. Nuclear explosions in May 1998 by both India and Pakistan resulted in weaponisation of this capability ,though it did not make any qualitative difference to the ongoing proxy war masterminded by Islamabad.

The human cost to India and Pakistan is tremendously high during the period. A large number of Pakistani and Indian soldiers were killed in 1998.Besides regular soldiers, Islamabad had militants from PoK, Afghanistan, Sudan, Bahrain, Turkey, Iran, Saudi Arabia, Yeman, Chachenya and Kazakhistan, who too were part and parcel of the proxy war. [12] According to Lt. General Shankar Prasad, 'about 15000 weapons captured from terrorists' were recycled among

Indian soldiers. In the recently published statistical data for the causalities in the state Jammu and Kashmir by insurgency from 1990 to 1998 is as under [13]:-

INDIAN POSITION

Army

Killed	-	959
Wounded	-	2871

Civilian

Killed	-	3241
Wounded	-	5992

PAK SOLDIERS

Killed	-	400
Apprehended	-	57

MERCENARIES

Killed	-	7776
Apprehended	-	24079
Surrendered	-	1823

Over All Recovery of Weapons during the period by India (1990-1998)[14]

(a)	AK-47 Rifle	-	13671
(b)	UMG/LMG	-	779
(c)	Sniper Rifle	-	498
(d)	Stenguns	-	27
(e)	Pistol	-	4889
(f)	SB/DB Guns	-	797
(g)	Anti-Personnel Mines	-	5422
(h)	Anti-Tank Mine	-	354
(j)	Hand Grenades	-	35547
(k)	RPGs	-	862

(l)	Explosive (kg)	-	11865
(m)	Radio Sets	-	1398
(n)	Ammunition	-	2693129

According to the defence publication, titled 'Proxy War' circulated by the HQ Northern Command at Udhampur, that mercenaries from 14 countries have been involved in the 10 years long 'proxy war' aided and abetted by Pakistan in Jammu and Kashmir.[15] These mercenaries belong to Afghanistan, Bahrain, Burma, Bangladesh, Chechanya, Iraq, Iran, Kazkhstan, Pakistan, Saudi Arabia, Sudan, Turkey and Yemen besides from PoK under operation 'Topac'. The report also said that, 1073 mercenaries of 13 countries have been killed between 1990 and 1998.[16]

(c) The Kargil Stand-off :1999

By sending heavily armed foreign mercenaries and army soldiers in civilian clothes across the Line of control (LoC) into Kargil, Drass and Batalic and J&K in the summer month of 1999, Pakistan had added a new dimension to its more than 10 years old 'proxy war' against India.[17] The three phases blueprint involved indoctrination, intrusion and sabotage by fifty columnists to be used as a major thrust by the Pakistani Army as had happened in Kargil. Pakistan began its trans-border terrorism against India with the support of JKLF and Hurriyat Conference. But, Indian intelligence network remained uninformed of the Pakistani preparation. Pakistan wanted to cut-off Kargil and Ladakh from the rest of J&K so as to cut –off Srinagar- Leh National Highway and to strengthen her position for talks with India in case that stage ultimately materialized.[18] Thereby, she would have claimed Kashmir valley, Doda, Rajouri and Kargil regions on the basis of religion. Pakistan also wanted to internationalize Kashmir issue so that she could involve the UN and the Western power for a settlement of Kashmir.[19]

(d) Operation 'Vijay' and post Kargil Situation:

A tense situation was developed in Drass, Batalik and Kargil sectors along the Line of Actual Control in the Ladakh region of J&K, while moving towards point Bajrang on May 8,1999, an Indian Army patrol saw some unusual movement in the area. The sources say that Pakistani soldiers assisted by 'mercenaries' occupied some heights on Indian side of the LoC after intruding 12 to 15 km inside Indian side of Kashmir territory. Many experts expressed that by April 1999, Pakistani troops and foreign mercenaries established themselves on the high mountain ridge lines at heights ranging between 15000 to 18000 feet, though the planning of operation appears to have moved into high gear by end of September 1998.[20] These ridge lines is inaccessible remote areas, which are mostly uninhabited and are patrolled and kept under surveillance by our troops during the summer months.

As a result, Operation 'Vijay' launched on May 26, 1999, to flush out Pakistani intruders from Kargil sector. Even as the Army and Air Force employed their synergies combat potential to eliminate the intruders and regain the territory occupied by them, it was important for the government to keep all channels of communication open and negotiate at the diplomatic and political levels with Pakistan to ensure that the Kargil conflict remains localized and Pakistan's military adventurism in Kargil is not allowed to escalate into a larger conflict.[21]

With the mounting pressure of world opinion and the relentless march of Indian troops which climaxed in the fall of strategic important Tiger Hill on July 4, 1999, Pak agreed to withdraw its forces from the Indian side of the LoC. On July14, 1999, the Kargil war ended when Pakistan, virtually withdrew all it forces from the Indian side of LoC. 'Operation Vijay' was superbly calibrated to limit military action to the Indian side of the LoC which included air strikes from Fighter Ground Attack (FGA) aircraft and Helicopter. [22] Undoubtedly, it had been a spectacular success of the Indian Army in which it stunned the enemy by pushing them back beyond the LoC in all the sectors in Kashmir in just 50 days however, during the operation 481 Indian soldiers had laid their lives, 1145 wounded and 2 are missing. Defence Minister of India, Mr. George Fernandes officially announced on July17, 1999, that the war in Kargil had ended, but New Delhi would not take any chances in future.

'Operation Vijay' succeeded in its goal of flushing out Pakistani troops and intruders from Kargil,and the Government of India could rightly claim it to be both a political and diplomatic feather in its cap. The sacrifices of our jawans united the entire nation and this ,in turn boosted the morale of our troops further. It was also a wake up call for our political military establishment and intellectual elite .

India had condemned Pakistan's insidious role in the recruitment, training and financing of mercenaries across the border over a decade. but this time with Kargil, the world community agreed with New Delhi's perception. This included important nations like USA, UK, and China This is the first time Pakistan was totally isolated from the international community.

Post- Kargil situation

In J&K the battle of wits between the militants and the security forces still continued and both tried to outmaneuver each other. Replying to question in the Lok Sabha, on April 18, 2000, Minister of States of Home, Mr. YCV Rao said, "in the post- Kargil phase, in J&K a total of 82 security personnel, 199 civilians and 245 militants were killed between January to March 2000 while the figure was 356 in 1999. a total of 1082 militants were killed in 1999 where, as civilian casualties were 821."[23] Not only that, the then US President Mr. Bill Clinton had visited Indian during March 2000, and was hoping that a solution could be found to curb the militancy ,but while his visit was to begin the militant struck at Chattisinghpora killing 35 Sikh. [24]The chronology of major killings in Jammu and Kashmir after Kargil Stand-off are as follows: [25]

20 June	1999	15 Hindu labourers killed in Anantanag.
19 July	1999	15 Hindus killed in Layata, Doda.
28 February	2000	5 Hindu drivers killed near Quzigund.
20 March	2000	35 Sikhs killed in Chattisinghpora.
01 August	2000	31 people including Amarnath yatris killed at Pahalgam.
01-2 August	2000	27 labourers gunned down in Qazigund and Acchabal, Anantnag district.
02 August	2000	7 family members killed in Kupwara and 11 Hinus killed in Doda district.
10 August	2000	14 people and 12 policemen were killed in Srinagar in a car bomb-blast.
22 November	2000	Militant killed 5 Sikh track drivers on Jammu-Srinagar Highway in Doda.
24 November	2000	Lashkar-e-Toiba killed 5 people in Doda.
01 October	2001	Militant attacked Assemble House at Sri nagar and killed 38 persons.
14 May	2002	30 family members and jawans killled in. K Kaluchwak
21 May	2002	Militant killed Abdul Gani Lone in a public meeting.
24 July	2002	21 labours killed near Jammu by Militants.

It has also been noted that, a large number of terrorist training camps were running still now across the border mainly by the Hizab-ul Mujahideen (HM), Harkat-ul-Mujahideen (HuM), .Lashkar-e-Toiba (LeT) Jaish-e-Mohammad (JeM) and Al-Badar. However, government had adopted a multi pronged approach, comprising of deployment of central para-military forces setting up a Border Observation Posts (BOPs) and provision a specialized equipment like night vision devices to the forces along the International Border to check infiltration and subversive activities.[26]

On the other side, Pakistan's Inter Service Intelligence (ISI) has asked several militant groups operating in J&K, to form Fidayan (suicide) groups to carry out subversion activities against security forces.[27] The sources said thousands of Kashmiri youth were waiting at Bagh in PoK, to cross over the state for carrying out subversive activities. ISI is trying to establish its bases in the Muslims dominated areas in the country to foment trouble and the area targeted by this game plan included Hyderabad, Western UP, North Kerala, HP, and TN beside Mumbai suburbs.[28]

According to the intelligence sources, Pakistan's ISI has chalked out a new eleven points strategy, including establishing a 'no fly zone'[29] within the Kashmir region, to step up militancy in J&K. The reports said, the ISI has directed the terrorists to create 'no fly zone' in the Kashmir region to keep Indian Air Force, fighter planes and helicopters out of that air space.[30] As per their plan and new strategy, the ISI will provide arms and ammunition and long range gun and mortar to the militants and any Indian air craft violating the 'no fly zone' would be shot down by anti-air guns.

The Kashmir policy of Pakistan has remain unchanged even after military take-over by the General Pervez Musharraf. Pakistan Chief Executive General Musharrafs offer to initiate talk with India on the Kashmir issue, at any time and any place to the Indian leaders was appreciated. But New Delhi made it clear that any talk would have to be on the basis of Simla Agreement and Lahore Declaration (February 22,1999). Further, New Delhi made it clear that for any fruitful dialogue , Islamabad has to recognize the in violability of LOC and end to hostile cross-border terrorist activities

During his visits abroad to countries South and West Asia , Pakistani General Parvez Musharraf said, 'we are ready to discuss on the Kashmir issue with India, 'at any time, any place and any level', but any permanent solution to the Kashmir issue should take into consideration hopes and aspirations of the Kashmiri people according to the United Nation resolutions related to the issue. Side by side, Islamic fundamentalists and militants, specially, Let and HuM warned Pakistan's military rulers against any peace talk with India and closing down of the militant camps under US pressure in the country saying '*jehad*' was the only way to settle the long pending Kashmir dispute.

PROXY WAR AND SPIRIT OF JIHAD

Kashmir has been the core contentious issues in all low-intensity wars that India has fought with Pakistan, beginning from Operation Gulmarg (1947) till the Kargil Stand-off (1999) and thereafter. While friction with Pakistan over Kashmir dates back to the time when India gained independence in 1947, however,, terrorist activities in the state are of much recent vintage. The death of Sheikh Mohammed Abdullah in 1982 created a vacuum in Kashmir's state politics and gradually increased the alienation between Kashmir and mainstream Indian polity and administration. Assembly election in 1987,widely believed to be rigged and manipulated, increased local discontent, practically among the Kashmir youth, who increasingly resorted to violent means of protest. As pointed out by a scholar, "terrorism is the half-thinking man's conditioned reflex to sustained oppression and lack of personal empowerment."[31] The gnawing feeling of despondency among the Kashmir people is underlined by some scholars as the root cause behind growth of insurgency in the state.

Terrorism reared its ugly head in Kashmir in December 1989, when the JKLF (Jammu and Kshmir Liberation Front) kidnapped Rubaiya Sayeed, daughter of Mufti Mohammad Sayeed, the Union Home Minister, and the present Chief Minister of Jammu and Kashmir. The government compromised with militants for securing the release of Rubaiya. Soon after, the state government collapsed in the face of widespread disturbance paving the way for imposition of President's Rule in the state.[32] The episode, underlining the growth of militancy in the state, was exploited to the hilt by Pakistan. The ISI (Inter Services Intelligence) of Pakistan began providing active backing to Kashmiri insurgents through the guerilla-warfare expertise gained in Afghanistan. The support, supply, and training system developed for aiding Afghans in their war against the Soviet was later on re-directed in support of the Kashmir struggle against Indian rule.

Quite apart from providing means of support for self-determination of Kashmir-which was the core issue of Pakistan's foreign policy, Islamabad was also seized of the problem if its lost erstwhile east Pakistan. Given the stark differences in economic and military capabilities between India and Pakistan, the latter has always been keen on fuelling low-intensity conflicts within the Indian state with the larger objective of destabilizing India's internal peace and harmony. Pakistan's involvement in the insurgency in Punjab in the early 1980s,in form of providing financial, military and other support to the militants, was established on several occasions. Kashmir was an exercise on similar lines. The disillusionment among the Kashmiri people with Indian rule and policies provided Pakistan the opportunity that it was looking for. What began as an indigenous movement for independence of Kashmir eventually became a larger crusade with distinct fundamentalist overtones for bringing Kashmir under Pakistan's control. While Islamabad does not raise the POK issue, it constantly brings New Delhi controlled part of Kashmir under international scrutiny inviting foreign intervention.

The fundamentalist dimension of terrorism in Kashmir has made the issue more vexing. This, of course, happened over a period of time, and has much to do with Pakistan's growing religious fundamentalism. During the 1980s, the then Pakistani President General Zia-ul-Haq actively promoted *madrassas* for garnering support of the clergy for his rule, and also for recruiting troops for fighting Soviets in Afghanistan.[33] Over time, these *madrassas* have evolved into seats of religious fundamentalism, encouraging their pupils to take up the cause of '*jihad*' for fighting Hindus in Kashmir and elsewhere, and also against other Muslims sects in Pakistan. They are usually funded privately without any kind of state intervention. According to official Pakistani estimates, 10 to 15 percent of the country's *madrassas* propagate extremist ideologies, and they are the supply -line for '*jihad*'.[34]

The spirit of '*jihad*' has captured the imagination of sections of the Pakistani society, particularly the unemployed youth, who consider it their 'spiritual duty' to carry out acts of terrorism against the enemies of their religion. The *madrassas*, on the other hand, aim to export their version of '*jihad*' to all corners of the world. The *Khudamudeen madrassa* trains students from Burma, Nepal, Chechnya, Bangladesh, Afghanistan, Yemen, Mongolia and Kuwait. Students from Uzbekistan, Tajikistan, Russia and Turkey also join *madrassas* receiving the knowledge for developing terrorist networks at home. [35] Terrorist outfits like *Al –Qaida* had been a potent mechanism for churning out terrorists motivated by religious fundamentalism which found congenial soil to strike deep roots within Pakistan. Organized capabilities of terrorism inspired by jihad hardly require reiteration after the September 11,2001 attacks on the US.

Over the years, Pakistan has emerged as both perpetrator and facilitator of terrorism. though its designs are principally aimed against India, terrorism aroused by religious fervor and honed in Pakistan, is now targeting a large section of the international community. While *madrassas* keep on imparting lessons in terrorism to eager recipients, Pakistan keeps on supporting the terrorists in various other forms. It assists the militants' passage into Kashmir and supports them economically and military.[36] By facilitating the activities of the irregulars in Kashmir, Islamabad aims to promote internal sectarianism within India and thereby frustrate prospects for peace through bilateral dialogues. In the process, however, Pakistan is being identified as an epicenter for international terrorism and tarnishing its own image in the comity of nations.

India estimates that about forty per cent of the militants in Kashmir today are Pakistanis or Afghan nationals and are-wise eighty per cent are teenagers.[37] According to further Indian, estimates, around 3000 to 4000 'mujahideens' are in Kashmir at any given time.[38] There is every possibility that the Taliban could be one of the constituents of the several mujahideens present in Kashmir.

The Talibans, a creation of America's CIA to fight the Soviets during the 1979 Soviet invasion of Afghanistan have now risen against their own creator. Despite the apparent demolition of the Taliban regime in Afghanistan, it would be naïve to assume that the Taliban influence has come to an end. On the country, the impact of Talibans on Pakistan's society and polity continues to be pronounced and interestingly enough, today even Dhaka is emerging as a 'nerve center' of terrorist activity.[39] This is all to indicate that there is an alarming rise in the ISI activity in the eastern region.[40] What Pakistan fails to realize, or probably overlooks, is the eventual aim of these militants, which is to convert Pakistan into a pure Islamic state and impose .A well known author quoted . "We wont stop- even if India gave us Kashmir. We'll [also] bring *jihad* here. There is already a movement here to make Pakistan a pure Islamic state. ... We want to see a Taiban-style regime here".[41] Terrorist groups like the Lashkar-I-Taiba has gone global in its operations today and announces their plan to 'plant Islamic flags in Delhi, Tel Aviv and Washington''. [42] The objective of the militants does not end at liberating Kashmir, which is merely a stepping-stone to their eventual goal.

PAKISTAN'S PRO – TERRORIST POLICY

In recent times, Pakistan has been trying hard to project a moderate face as a nation. The mounting international pressure (particularly that of the US) which has come down hard on terrorism and religious fundamentalism, subsequent to the terrorist attack on Indian Parliament on December 13, 2001, forced General Musharraf to adopt reconciliatory postures. Addressing the nation on January 12,2002, he promised to take his country on the road to moderate Islam. In a later address on June 6,2002, he pledged to the US administration to stop cross-border terrorism permanently and visibly, and also promised to dismantle terrorist infrastructure in terms of training camps etc. While banning of a few military outfits, and arrest of some hardliners, followed General Musharraf's pronouncements, cross-border terrorism continued unabated. Despite Pakistan's contention that infiltration has stopped along the Line of Control (LOC)— the General's views, "nothing is happening on the LOC and this has been recognized by everyone that infiltration has been minimized"[43] — However, it remained unconvincing since terrorist outfits like Al-Madina, Babur Hind Force, Azad Jehad etc. continued to operate in different parts of Kashmir. These groups are supposedly of LeT origin. According to a report conveyed by the Government of Kashmir to the Union Home Ministry, phone and wireless messages of these groups underline the regular contact between themselves on "aiding cross-border terror, direction and strategy of operations, increasing violence in the valley before the polls, discouraging people from going to the polls"[44]

While President Musharraf continues to suggest that cross-border terrorism between Pakistan and India no longer exists, he does, also, reveal his inability to check the same. During an interview to the CNN in September 2002, he mentioned that "the border with Indian was treacherous with high mountains and it was not possible to seal the border and give a guarantee over infiltration." [45] The General's submissions, despite his 'radical' addresses earlier during the year, cast doubts upon the sincerity of the ruling regime in Pakistan for ending terrorism. It is also worth pondering as to whether cessation of support to the Kashmiri militants was either a desirable, or a politically attractive step to take. Distancing the Pakistani administration completely from the Taliban, or the *Al-Qaida* and its ilk, could entail heavy costs for General Musharraf, in terms of erosion of support among Pakistan's radical elements.[46] Simultaneously, turning off the spigot on the Kashmiri militants, though not tantamount to political suicide as some analysts in the

US would suggest, could certainly cost the General Musharraf support among his ruling politico- military- diplomatic coteris.[47]

Pakistan's exploitation of the Kashmir issue still holds considerable appeal within the country's ruling elite due to the emotive sensitivities of the matter. General Musharraf's insistences that the insurgents in Kashmir were 'freedom fighters' and not terrorists – even after banning outfits like Jaish-e-Muhammad and the Lashkar-e-Taiba- was indicative of his regime's unwillingness to abandon its support for cross-border terrorism in Kashmir.[48] The reasons behind Pakistan' eagerness to remain involved in Kashmir are also comprehensible. Pakistan is aware of the remote possibility of its emerging victorious in the event of a full- fledged conventional war against India. At the same time, despite both the countries possessing nuclear capabilities, a nuclear confrontation is also highly unlikely, since the international community would ensure that such a confrontation never occurs. In the past, US initiatives have successfully thwarted imminent conflicts between India and Pakistan. Ideally, therefore, Pakistan would like to keep the Indian forces occupied in Kashmir in low-intensity conflicts just as the Afghan mujahideen had kept the Soviet troops engaged in Afghanistan.[49] It is also worth considering as to whether Pakistan is at all interested in a lasting solution of the Kashmir issue, since, it wants to frustrate India's ambition to emerge as a regional power[50] and would hardly be inclined to normalization of bilateral relations.

Despite the clear double standards that Pakistan maintains on abatement of terrorism, General Musharraf's public pronouncements, in terms of the addresses refered to earlier, were indeed remarkable. While international pressure could have been instrumental behind the General's statements, the possibility of changing dynamics of the international strategic environment having impacted his postures also cannot be ruled out. The gradually improving bilateral ties between India and the US, India's commitment to the global war against terrorism and the US appreciation of India's role, have probably forced Pakistan to adopt an ' official' anti-terrorism stance. Further, the US ambassador to India, Robert Blackwill's direct comparison between the attacks in India (December 13, 2001) and the US (September 11, 2001) was seen by many strategic analysts as US endorsement of actions on part of India similar to those undertaken by the US in Afghanistan.[51]

Since Islamabad also claims itself to be frontline ally of the US in the crusade against terrorism, and did live up to the claim by allowing liberal use of its territory during the military campaign in Afghanistan in November 2001, promulgation of domestic policies in line with this broader commitment would have certainly raised its stock among the international community. Any stand, taken to the contrary, would have helped India in assuming the dominant status in the region and securing greater support of the US and the West.

The hardlliners in Pakistan, however, do wish to break away from Washington's global war on terrorism; and opposes the Pakistani government's support for Washington in tracking down Osama-bin-Laden. While Laden remains elusive for the world at large, Pakistan's success in keeping Kashmir away from the mainstream of Indian society by supporting terrorism in the Valley seems to have run into trouble with the successful conclusion of the democratic process of assembly elections in the state. While the international community hailed the assembly elections in Kashmir, Pakistan tried to derail the election process through various means. A specially prepared bulletin reported, "these are ham lecterns. Plebiscite and no fraudulent elections is the demand of the Kashmiri people."[52] The assassination of the Hurriyat leader Abdul Gani Lone in the run up to the elections, allegedly masterminded by the ISI, was an attempt to refrain the common people from participating in the polls. However, the success of the elections not only symbolizes revivals of democratic institutions and ideals in Kashmir, but also undermines Pakistan's demand for plebiscite in the Valley.

INDIA'S POLICY OF PROTEST AND COMBATING TERRORISM

India has been consistently highlighting the need for a unified international response to terrorism, which has today assumed global proportions, and is challenging established societies, institutions and governments. As far as India is concerned, enough evidence has been collected, and demonstrated to the rest of the world, regarding the links between terrorist groups operating from the Indian soil, and those in other countries. The role or Pakistan in cementing the nexus between different terrorist groups of various geographical origins has also been pointed out on various occasions.

In voicing its views on terrorism, India has been taking pains to point out the vulnerability of democracies, in particular, to the menace of terrorism. It has called for concerted global action to counter terrorism and for ensuring enactment of prohibitive measures, like imposition of punitive sanctions against states responsible for sponsoring terrorism in various ways. The Government of India has actively supported the declaration adopted by the UN General Assembly on measures to eliminate international terrorism(1994) and the International Convention adopted by the UN General Assembly to suppress terrorist bombings (1997). Indian has also actively associated with resolutions in the United Nations Human Rights Commission(UNHRC) that condemn terrorism as a prime violator of human rights.

Despite Pakistan's claims to the contrary,. India maintain that cross- border terrorism continues unabated within India, and Pakistan's involvement in the terrorist acts is evident. It recognizes that the entire network of terrorism patronized by Pakistan aims to dismember Kashmir ,which is an 'integral part of India.' While accepting Kashmir as a problem that emerged after the invasion in 1947, Indian rejects the contention that Kashmir's status is "disputed". General Musharraf, on the other hand, reiterates that Kashmir is the "core" issue between New Delhi and Islamabad.[53]

Indian has been urging the international community to pressurize Pakistan to end cross border terrorism by stopping infiltration and dismantling militant camps on its soil and in Pakistan-occupied Kashmir(POK). It is interesting to note that for the first time the international community has viewed the India-Pakistan stand-off seriously, after Pakistan indulged in nuclear blackmail ,threatening to use nuclear weapons if it was pushed too far, in the aftermath of mobilization of troops on the borders following the recent Kaluchak incident of May 14,2002.It was feared that in the face of limited strikes on military camps in POK by India, it would "definitely provoke a retaliation by Pakistan and the *situation can spin out of control*" (emphasis added).[54] Some strategic analysts in India, however, think otherwise. According to this school of thought, 'war' was never on the cards. They believe that deployment of troops along the border in the recent past were exercises by India aiming to raise the cost of terrorism for Pakistan, and forcing the US increase its pressure on Pakistan. [55]

Pakistan is aware that as in the case of a conventional war, in the event of a nuclear war too, it has little chance for survival. It is precisely in the light of this knowledge that nuclear deterrence ensured that there would not be a full scale nuclear war.[56] The eventual outcome was to use force short of overlay military confrontation between forces of either side, which included artillery exchanges, apart from use of mortars and small arms, but didn't extend to crossing the LOC (incidentally, however, Pakistan had crossed the LOC during the Kargil Stand-off). [57]

India believes that terrorism is indivisible and there cannot be double standards in combating it. The United Nations Security Council (UNSC) resolution 1373 clearly indicates that there is one definition of terrorism under international law, which includes cross-border terrorism. This resolution requires all States to prevent those who finance, plan, facilitate, or commit terrorist acts, from using their respective territories for those purposes against other countries and their citizens. India is of the view that resolution 1373, and its follow up 1390- must be implemented fully by all concerned. It is mentionable in this context that a resolution against terrorism was adopted at CICA. Almaty, which specifically denies any role of terrorism in relation to demands for separatism, thereby making terrorism a non-justifiable instrument for furthering separatist causes in examples like Chechnya and Jammu and Kashmir.[50]

India has decided to confront cross border terrorism decisively. In its attempt to fight cross-border terrorism, India has instituted a new legislation, Prevention of Terrorist Activities (POTA), in place of the earlier Prevention of Terrorism Ordinance (POTO). According to India's Home Minister, Mr. .L.K. Advani, "Our objective is to fight terrorism, especially state-sponsored cross-border terrorism, which is even more dangerous that open war.[59] POTA has been framed in the light of India's objective to fight "cross- border terrorist war". Commenting on POTA, the Indian Home Minister mentioned that India was obligated to have such a law in the statute as part of its commitment to the "anti-terror coalition", and to comply with the UN Security Resolution 1373.[60] The US State Department has hailed the passage of the law, calling it a "more effective tool "to fight terrorism, and even pronouncing that it was within "constitutional bounds".[61] The law, however, has met with considerable opposition from various quarters within India, with questions been raised over its institutionalization, drawbacks and misgivings.

India appreciates the understanding, support, and solidarity, demonstrated by the international community in favour of its struggle against terrorism. The international public opinion appears to be largely sympathetic towards the Indian cause. India's stand against terrorism, however, would be ultimately vindicated if the international community realizes that weeding out terrorism, and isolating its state patrons, like Pakistan, is not merely in India's national interests, but is also essential for carrying forward the global campaign against terrorism, and protecting democratic institutions and societies from the threats of terrorist acts. But for securing this objective, it is important for the world community to first arrive at an agreeable definition of terrorism.

TO CONCLUDE

Comprehension of the factors behind cross-border terrorism in the Indian sub-continent inevitably highlights the problems surrounding Kashmir. Kashmir has been instrumental behind increased volatility of the South Asian region, demands for international scrutiny and intervention, as well as the ending of unabated terrorist activities.

The events of 9/11,2001, drove home the point that terrorism is a 'live threat' for the international community. which has, in a way, facilitated Indian's struggle against terrorism. Before September 11, cross-border terrorism was often dismissed as an internal concern of India. Events of 9/11, and thereafter, have vindicated India's stand. It was also firmly established that Afghanistan, under the Taliban regime and with Pakistan's tacit support, had become the most fertile breeding ground for terrorists.

The war against terrorism, however, doesn't end at the displacement of the Taliban. On the contrary, terrorist attacks in India and elsewhere (e.g. Bali in Indonesia) are evidence of sustenance of terrorist networks like *Al-Qaida.* while the Taliban might not be having a national base any longer, their influence continues to prevail upon significant sections of certain societies. Pakistan is probably the best example in this regard. The international public opinion, led by the US, seems to have run into crossroads over the likely means for weeding out terrorism from Pakistan. On one hand, the world is aware of the significant influence exerted by fundamental religious elements on the Pakistani society, and the impact of this influence on spread of terrorism in Kashmir and the rest of the world. At the same time, the dominant global view, once again propagated by the US, seems to be in favour of handling out 'soft' treatment of Pakistan, in view of the arguably 'crucial' role it can play in suppressing terrorism, since Pakistan is believed to have insider knowledge about terrorist activities.

The above stand reiterates the double standard being adopted by the global community for fighting terrorism. As far as India is concerned, apart from its frustration at the apparent reluctance of the international community to take precipitate action against the perpetrators of terrorism, it is also bothered about the ease with which Pakistan is able to manipulate the international community for securing its own benefits. As recent events indicate, outbreak of terrorism has often led to development of war like situation in the subcontinent with both India and Pakistan mobilizing troops along the border.

However, several wars have never actually materialised due to the quick intervention of the international community for diffusing the situation. Evidently the later is worried about the possibility of an eventual nuclear confronatation between the two neighbours, and does everything to prevent the possibility. This pattern of response perfectly suits Pakistan. It known that it can keep on patronizing terrorism without any serious consequences, like war, since the international community would never permit such a development. In fact, in this regard, Pakistan also has the option of resorting to nuclear blackmail,. which it did successfully during the latest border crisis in May-June 2002.

To add to India's frustrations further, the US, European Union, and the Group of Eight, have actually acknowledged Pakistan's export of terror to India, and have urged Islamabad to put a 'permanent stop to terrorist activity' and to clamp down on 'cross-border terrorism', a term used usually only by New Delhi. [62] However, the pressure was short-lived and soon, India began to be pressurized for opening dialogue with Pakistan.

Strategic analysts believe that a subtle US policy shift has been discernible in the recent months. Washington no longer insists, like it did till the last summer that Pakistan 'permanently' and 'verifiably' end cross-border terrorism to facilitate consequential dialogue with India. In a reversal of position, it calls for 'simultaneity' ——India opening dialogue with Islamabad, as America 'in parallel' seeks to persuade its client regime Pakistan there to cease the export of terror.[63]

Predicaments in the current scenario are not limited to India only. President Musharraf is walking a knife's edge in his domestic constituency as he tries to keep a deeply polarized country from tearing itself apart, now that his regime has pledged full support to the US in its war against terrorism. Musharraf was quick to realize that Islamabad stood the risk of getting alienated from the international community if it tried to defend the Talibans. He even confirmed to his nation that had he not offered the bases and other facilities to the US troops, India would have done it, and that would have posed severe threats to Pakistan's nuclear programme and stance on the 'disputed' territory of Kashmir.[64]

The following are the broad conclusions that emerge in the light of the issues involved in the current scenario :

Cross-border terrorism is a global phenomenon and need to resolved through a multilateral approach. Unilateral solutions can't solve the problem. There is concrete evidence of terrorist organizations shedding their loose and diffused structure and getting increasingly organized. The problem therefore demands collective action.[65] International cooperation must be directed at cutting out and terminating crucial lifelines of terrorist groups state sponsorship, refuge and sanctuary, financial support including nexus with narco-trafficking, and arms training and supply.[66] Action against terrorism should be both preventive and deterrent. This would require enhanced cooperation requiring our collective purpose of combating terrorism in all its forms, decisively and everywhere.[67] Essential to such international cooperation would be sharing of perceptions, experiences, intelligence, etc, which USA and other advanced nations technology-wise could be the possible agency to do the needful.

1. Specific strategic interests of major world powers could, occasionally, prove more relevant in fighting terrorism.. Hence it is important for major world power to 'engage' certain countries in place of other countries with which they are fighting terrorism. In the context, India's terrorism problem is presently on the periphery of the global war on terror. It would be interesting to observe how the international community decides to tackle this problem of global dimension in future, and how Pakistan 'engages' the great powers, who in turn would focus on other pressing issues.
2. The international community presently has a piecemeal approach towards terrorism. The would make the menace thrive. Demolishing the Taliban and Al Qaeda in Afghanistan has not put an end to terrorism.
3. The time has probably come for India to adopt carrot and stick policy in its fight against terrorism. It is important to proceed without relying on the response of the international community. This is imperative since the cost of terrorism for India is turning out to be exceedingly high. Russia's handling of the recent hostage crisis in a Moscow theater can be an useful example in this regard. India should also learn form its past mistakes, like striking deals with terrorists for releasing Rubaiyya Syaeed in 1989, which are inimical to prevention of the malaise.
4. Kashmir would continue to remain a crisis flashpoint till both neighbors show the political will to talk. While the international community wants the two South Asian powers to talk, the chances are slim, since Pakistan remains 'obsessed' with Kashmir and wants it to be the 'core' issue in any kind of discussion with India. The latter, on the other hand, would talk only after Pakistan gives up supporting cross-border terrorism.
5. Latest political developments and election results in Pakistan

are hardly encouraging. Power will, in all probability, lie with President Musharraf, the Army and the clergy and things would remain the same as before.

REFERENCES :

1. Dr. H.K. Srivastava, "Proxy War-Role of Indian army", The Chronicle, 23 March 1999.
2. Ibid.
3. Ibid.
4. Ibid.
5. Ibid.
6. K.K. Nanda, 'Conquering Kashmir – A Pakistani Obsession', Lancers Books. New Delhi, 1996 p. 297.
7. Jagmohan, 'My Frozen Turbulence in Kashmir', (New Delhi: Allied Publishing Limited), 1991 p.373.
8. K.K. Nanda, p. 305
9. Jag Mohan, p. 403.
10. VK Nair, 'Low-Intensity conflict – J&K;', *USI Journal*, Jul-Sep 1998-, p. 408.
11. Ibid. pp. 414-415
12. Dr. H.K. Srivastava, "Proxy War-Role of Indian army," *The Chronicle*, 23 March 1999
13. Ibid.
14. Ibid.
15. Post-Kargil developments, New Panorama of India and World, October 1999. P. 12.
16. Ibid.
17. Gurmeet Kanwal, "Pakistan Upgradess Proxy War", *The Excelsior*, 21 June 1999.

18. Hasim Qureshi, "Mounting Tension in Kargil Sector", *the Kashmir Times*, 19 June 1999.
19. Ibid
20. Gurmeet Kanwal, "Pakistan Upgrades Proxy War", *the Excelsior*, 21 June 1999.
21. Ibid.
22. Ibid.
23. 'Daily *the Excelsior'*, 19 April 2000.
24. Anita Kanungo, "Peace Pangs., *The Hindustan Times*, New Delhi, 06 August 2000.
25. Chronology of massacres in J&K, '*The Hitavada'* (Nagpur daily paper) o3 August 2000.
26. '*The Kashmir Times'*, 19 April 2000. Seventy kilometers of the 182 kilometers long international border have been fenced and flood lighted in Jammu border and this will stop infiltration and smuggling form Pakistan. *See theHitavada (Nagpur) 25 April,2003*
27. 'ISI asks for Fidayan groups to carry out militant activity' *The Excelsior*, 8 January 2000.
28. ISI plan, 'No fly Zone' in Kahmir, '*The Asian Age'*, 19 April 2000.
29. 'Pakistan's continuous calls for 'Jehad', Daily *the Excelsior*, 30 April 2000.
30. 'No talk till Pak ends hostility', *The Tribune*. 21 January 2000.
31. Shaukat Quadir, "The Concept of International Terrorism : An Interim Study of South Asia", *Round Table,* (360), 2001, p. 333.
32. Dennis Kux, *The United States and Pakistan, 1947 – 2000: Disenchanted Allies*(New York : Oxford University Press, 20001) p. 305.

33. Sterm, no. 2, pp. 118-19.
34. Ibid. p. 120.
35. Ibid. p, 123.
36. Jessica Sterm, "Pakistan 's Jihad culture" Foreign Affairs, vol. 79, no. 6, Nov-Dec. 2000 , p. 116.
37. Ibid. p. 118.
38. Ibid.
39. "Pakistan High Commission in Dhaka is ISI nerve Centre : Sinha", the *Times of India*, 28 November 2002.
40. Ibid.
41. A harkat operative responds to the author Jessica Sterm, no. 2, p. 121.
42. No. 2. p. 124.
43. Statement by General Musharraf in an interview to the CNN in September, see B. Muralidhar, "Nothing Happening on LOC : Musharraf", *The Hindu,* 17 September 2002.
44. Despite Ban, LeT factions strike terror in Kashmir",the *Time of India,* 11 August 2002.
45. B. Muralidhar, "Nothing Happeining of LOC : Musharraf", *The Hindu,* 17 September 2002.
46. Tinku Varadarajan, "Overgeneralization : The Case Against Pakistan's Disctators", WSJ. Com opinion Journal, 20 November 2001. as cited by Sumit Ganguly, "Indian and Pakistan in the shadow of Afghanistan', *Current History,* vol. 101, no 654, Apri 2002, p. 148.
47. Sumit Ganguly, " India and Pakishan in the shadow of Afghanistan", *Current History,* vol. 101, no. 654 April 2002, p. 148.
48. Ibid.

49. "Inside the Mind of the Dictator", *Indian today*, 3 June 2002,p.44.

50. Ibid.

51. "The tragic event that occurred on Thursday and perpetrated by terrorists was no different in its objective from the terror attacks in the US on september 11". Sec "India,US together in Fighting Terror: Robert Blackwill", 14 December 2001, *http://www.rediff.com/news/2001/dec/14parl10.htm.*

52. Zaffar Abbas, "Pakistan Shuns Kashmir Poll', *BBC News*, 17 September 2002. htt;//news.bbc.co.uk//2/low/south_asia/ 2259458.stm.

53. "Advani Raises Cross-border Terrorism", *The Hindus*, 15 July 2001.

54. "Khalid Mahmood, "Any strike by India will provoke war", 21 May 2002. http;//www.tribuncindia. com/2002/20020533/ world.htm#.1

55. K. Subrahmanyan, "Courting confusion; 'War' was never on the Cards", the *Times of India*, 24 June 2002.

56. Ibid.

57. Ibid.

58. Brajesh Mishra, Statement by National Security Adviser of India, Moscow, June 5, 2002, http//www.meadev.inc.in/ speeches/stmt_brajesh-5june2002.htm

59. "POTA- The Latest Black Law', http//www.geocites.com/ aipsg/charcha/ May2002/alok_pota.htm.

60. Ibid.

61. Ibid.

62. Brahma Chellaney, "Learning from a Dud", *The Hindustan Times*, 22 November 2002.

63. Ibid.

64. Ahmed Rashid, *Dispatches*, 27 September 2001. http://www.bard.edu/hrp/Hrresponses/terrorism/dispatches.world.htm.

65. The LeT and the JeM are registered organizations in Pakistan provided with official patronage till 26. December 2001. Kshitij Prabha, "Terror Enterprise : Organization, Infrastructure and Resources", *Strategic Analysis*, vol. 25, no. 9, December 2001, p 1047.

66. POTA, no. 59.

67. Ibid.

10

India and Pakistan : Prospects for Peace

Nalini Kant Jha

The Indo-Pak equation has changed to such an extent in recent years that, apart from asking the familiar question whether Pakistan can still threaten India seriously, one also asks whether the chances of normal relations between the estranged neighbours have improved, and if they have, whether in due course can one expect long-term peace. This question has assumed added significance in view of Indian Prime Minister, Atal Behari Vajpayee's latest offer of friendship to Pakistan and reciprocal gesture on the part of Pakistani leaders. India has announced resumption of air links with Pakistan and reposting of its High Commissioner in Islamabad, which was withdrawn in the wake of Pakistan-sponsored terrorist attack on Indian Parliament in December 2001. Though this underlines political message of hope, yet if both the neighbours do not seize the qualitative opportunity and take more salutary steps than before to de-escalate the abnormal tensions in their relations, the war cloud could gather once again.

It is therefore high time for both the neighbours in general and the victim of cross border terrorism, India, in particular to utilize the favourable climate for quickly moving towards peace building in South Asia. At the same time, India cannot afford to lower its guard in view of its past experiences in dealing with Pakistan. We propose to discuss in this paper the indicators of peace between India and Pakistan and suggest policy frame for moving towards peace without risking India's security. But before evaluating the prospects for peace in South Asia, it is pertinent to recapitulate the recent developments leading to India-Pakistan stand off since December 2001.

THE THREE-PRONGED INDIAN STRATEGY:

As we approach the crossroad in India-Pakistan relations, the reasons behind India's largest-ever military mobilization need to be recalled. To put it briefly, the Indian Government's decision that the December 13 attack was the last straw on the camel's back was not surprising. For more than a decade New Delhi had just chosen to absorb the pain from Islamabad's strategy of bleeding it through a thousand cuts. Convinced that India would not be able to retaliate it for supporting cross-border terrorism, Pakistan believed that it had a free hand in fomenting violence across the border in Jammu and Kashmir and take it to high value targets in rest of the nation as well.

More significantly, attack on Parliament came after Pakistan's repeated betrayal of several peace initiatives by the Vajpayee administration. As against a widely held expectation about pursuit of an unduly tough line in dealing with Pakistan by the BJP-led Government, it actually exhibited on the contrary a remarkable willingness to travel away from the "beaten path" to explore the possibility of bringing a measure of peace and civility in relations with Pakistan and within Jammu and Kashmir. This is evident from the fact that despite Pakistan's rebuffing of Prime Minster, Atal Behari Vajpayee's Lahore peace initiative through Kargil perfidy in 1999, he took yet another bold peace initiative by implementing a unilateral ceasefire in Kashmir in the Islamic holy month of *Ramzan* in November 2000.[1] Besides, he invited the Pakistan President, General Pervez Musharraf, for talks in the historical town of Agra in July 2001.[2] Unfortunately, Islamabad responded to these peace initiatives by engineering attacks on the Jammu and Kashmir Sate Assembly on 1 October; on the Indian Parliament House on December 13, 2001.

As India could not forever continue to absorb the pains of this support to the so called "freedom struggle," which is nothing but an euphemism for Pakistan's encouragement and abetment to terrorist violence in Kashmir, the attack on the Parliament house obliged India into confronting the source of the threat once and for all. Accordingly, New Delhi mobilized its troops on the India-Pakistan borders to demonstrate its resolve to fight the war against terrorism at all cost. Being a mature and responsible nation having understanding of the implications of a war between two nuclear armed neighbours and its international ramifications, New Delhi, however, and rightly decided to give diplomacy one more chance even while preparing for exercise of the last option, i.e., war.[3] That is why, even while readying its defence forces for military action after the attack on Parliament, New Delhi did give priority to diplomatic offensive including recalling of its High commissioner from Islamabad, slicing down the presence of Pakistani staff in its High Commission in New Delhi, terminating the New Delhi-Lahore bus service as well the *Samjhauta* Express, withdrawing permission to Pakistan to fly its aircrafts through the Indian sky, and demanding the extradition of 20 persons accused of committing various terrorist acts in India. New Delhi also demanded from Pakistan an effective action against Pakistan based terrorist groups such as *Lashkar-e-Taiba* (LeT) and *Jaish-e-Mohammad*.

As the Vajpayee Government did not expect any voluntary action on the part of Pakistan, it banked on the moral indignation of the international community, apart from mobilizing its military forces. It made intensive consultation with leaders of important countries such as the US, Britain, Russia, Japan, and China, etc.

This three-pronged Indian strategy—military build up, mobilizing international pressure, and mounting bilateral pressure on Pakistan produced certain results. These moves not only obliged the Pakistan President, Pervez Musharraf, to condemn religious extremism in his open address to this country on January 12, 2002, but also to ban certain terrorist outfits including LeT and JeM. Besides, he arrested hundreds of terrorists and detained their kingpin Maulana Masood Azhar, though as a balancing exercise he refused to hand over any Pakistani national demanded by India and declared the Kashmir issue as forming the blood stream of every Pakistani.

But it soon became apparent that the Pakistani President was either unwilling or incapable or both to control the extremist forces radiating out of Pakistani soil against India. The Musharraf regime's decision to soon free the detained extremists on the ground that no charges could be sustained against them was indicative of this reality. This emboldened the terrorist groups to first attack the Raghunath temple in Jammu and then to commit the gruesome massacre of Indians including 22 Army personnel at Kaluchak in Jammu on May 14; and to kill a moderate and peace-inclined Kashmiri leader, Abdul Gani Lone in the same month of 2002. Islamabad on its part conducted a series of missile tests and reportedly shifted some of its forces deployed along Pakistan-Afghanistan borders to the eastern side bordering India to deter the Indian forces and warn the international community about implications of any Indian move to attack the terrorist camps operating within Pakistan. The Pakistani forces also resorted to heavy shelling across the Indian side of LoC forcing India forces to return the firing.

Besides, President Musharraf chose to address his country on May 27 in which he simply declined Pakistan's involvement in cross border terrorism in India and appealed the global community to "ask India to move towards normalisation of relations" with his country.[4] This was quite contrary to his earlier address of January 12 assuring the world community to dismantle the terrorist networks active within Pakistan. Not surprisingly India described this statement as "mere verbal denials" about Pakistan's "lethal export of terrorism." The then Indian Foreign Minister, Jaswant Singh, described this statement as "both highly disappointing and dangerous."[5] The various spokesmen of the Indian Government, too, clearly declared, "India cannot be penalized for ever for its patience." India's expulsion of Pakistan's High Commissioner in New Delhi, Ashraf Jehangir Qazi, reflected India's cascading anger and a strong sense of frustration over Pakistan's belligerent behaviour.

After the Kaluchak massacre, India and Pakistan were thus on the verge of fighting the fifth war with much more devastating potentials than the earlier ones. As indicated at the outset, while the Anglo-American pressures - beginning with South Asia trip of the British Foreign Secretary, Jack Straw, followed by visits to this region by US Deputy Secretary of State, Richard Armitage, and the US Defence Secretary, Donald Rumsfeld, could defuse the escalating crisis and General Musharraf once again promised this time to the visiting US Defence Secretary that he will permanently dismantle the infrastructure of terrorist net-wok in Pakistan, Islamabad has not implemented its commitment.

This is evident from continued terrorist violence in India including the attack on Akshardham temple in Gujarat in August 2002, killings and intimidation to disrupt the Jammu and Kashmir Assembly election in September 2002, the massacre of Kashmiri Pundits at Nadimarg village in the troubled state in March 2003, and attack on Jammu and Kashmir Radio station in April 2003. This shows that the fragile peace now obtaining in South Asia can get disturbed and Prime Minister Vajpayee's third bold attempt to make peace with Pakistan after failure of his Lahore and Agra mission may fail again due to the Musharraf regime's unwillingness/incapacity to control the influx of terrorists into the Indian side of LoC and their subsequent acts of violence. In the nine years that Pakistan has succeeded in artificially prolonging the violence in Kashmir, more that 9,000 Kashmiri civilians lost their lives at the hands of their self-proclaimed liberators. Despite—or perhaps because of—

this, as the MORI poll in April-May 2002 revealed, even fewer Kashmiris (6 per cent) are prepared to contemplate their future as Pakistanis.[6] Under the circumstances, an amicable solution of the Kashmir dispute through negotiation will be feasible only when Pakistan comes to terms with this reality. Till it does so, the threat of war between India and Pakistan will persist.

INDICATORS OF PEACE

Paradoxical though it may appear, even as the cloud of war has not altogether disappeared from the South Asian horizon and India needs military preparedness to cope with that eventuality, prospects for peace is not bleak. One can discern signals for peace making at both international and domestic levels.

Taking the international milieu first, it should obvious to even a naïve observer of international relations that after the Cold War much has changed in great power equation with India and Pakistan. From a "zero-sum" approach during the Cold War, the Western countries in general and the US in particular, are developing their separate policies towards the sub-continental rivals on the basis of the inherent interests in both countries. India's rapid economic growth and liberalisation programme in the 1990s, influence of the 'Indo-American' community in the US, display of responsible international behaviour on the part of India after Pokharan-II, America's pressing need for India's software professionals, Washington's interest in peace after the Cold War to enable its citizens to enjoy in the safe heaven of home, etc., have motivated Washington to extend an accommodative approach towards India.[7] On the other hand, the endemic financial crisis in Pakistan has begun to differentiate the Western policies towards the two nations. Pakistan's drift towards extremist policies has also alarmed the major powers and many of Islamabad's neighbours. Not surprisingly, the Kargil crisis saw an important shift in the US approach, which forced Pakistan to unconditionally and unilaterally withdraw from across the LOC. Since then the US has argued that the status quo in Kashmir cannot be changed by use of force.

Accordingly, intervention by international community led by the US in any India-Pakistan conflict has now become as certain as day following night. As the industrialized counties of the West led by the US have a vested interest in international peace and stability in the drastically altered milieu of the post Cold War world,[8] Washington and other countries have repeatedly stepped in to prevent India-Pakistan war by activating their diplomatic channels. The terrorist attacks on the symbols of American and Indian sovereignty respectively on September 11 and December 13 2001 have all the more heightened American concerns about sources of international terrorism inside Pakistan. Although Washington's interest in retaining Pakistan's support in its war against Taliban and Al-Qaeda has dampened its condemnation of Pakistan's support to cross border terrorism, still the US has been under pressure to face up to the question of Pakistan's support to terrorism in terms of a consistent application of its own proclaimed principles as well as the Indian threat to go to war. That is why, the global community led by the US put considerable pressure on Pakistan to stop using terror as a means of foreign policy and thereby prevented fifth India-Pakistan war after the terrorist attacks on Indian Parliament on 13 December and the Kaluchak massacre of May 14.

Moreover, as a lasting peace process is in America's own interest, Washington would not longer want to expend diplomatic energies every six months to manage a crisis and turn its back on the region for the next six months. The Bush administration is therefore forced into a substantive effort aimed at conflict resolution, given its new political stakes in the region. This is evident from American efforts for the success of Vajpayee's peace initiatives in the summer of 2003.

An attitudinal change on the part of India, which now perceives the US participation as the key to a different future in the subcontinent, has also contributed to a major American role in the South Asian peace process. New Delhi's intense interactions with the major world powers in general and the US in particular both after attack on Parliament, and Kaluchak and Nadimarg massacres indicate that it has gradually realised the hollowness of assumption that the West will inevitably be hostile towards this country in any dispute between India and Pakistan. Unlike in the past, when India strove to prevent American involvement in India-Pakistan conflicts, it now, on the contrary, realises that the Pakistan army, which has developed the cheap and effective instrument of cross border terrorism to bleed this country, will use every trick in the book to avoid giving it up unless the Bush administration makes it clear to Islamabad that the costs of persisting with that instrument are not worth Pakistan's while. It is heartening to note that the after the Iraq war, America is once again turning its attention towards the facilitation of negotiations between India and Pakistan.

Internally, a window of opportunity for bringing the Kashmiri people back into our fold has opened once again. The Kashmiris have turned away from Pakistan after the latest instance of the trampling of democracy in that country in the guise of referendum. Besides, they cannot but take note of the fact that India has demonstrated in Kargil and military build up after December 13 and May 14 that it is prepared to make any sacrifice to retain every inch of territory on its side of the Line of Control (LoC). Besides, the BJP leadership, particularly because of political space it occupies, is in a better position to help evolve a broad-based consensus in this regard. Finally, though there is revival of indigenous insurgency, the fatigue from violence that set in the mid-1980s still persists. Though the killing of Abdul Gani Lone has silenced an important voice in favour of moderation and peace in Kashmir, this reflects panic among the hardliners rather than their confidence.

The above-mentioned developments clearly call for concerted efforts on the part of both New Delhi and Islamabad to turn away from the past bickering and seize the opportunity knocking at their doors. However, since the present paper focuses on India's policies, we shall briefly discuss in the next two sections external and internal dimensions of efforts required on the part of India to normalize its relations with Pakistan, without which it cannot play a meaningful role in international politics.

ROAD MAP FOR THE FUTURE

Having come out with a reasonable success from a dangerous and tricky strategic manoeuvre, the Vajpayee administration must now prepare the nation for a substantive engagement with Pakistan. But having failed twice at Lahore and Agra, will the Vajpayee regime be lucky third time in finding a basis for a peaceful coexistence with Pakistan? While only time can answer this question, certain precautions to be maintained by New Delhi in its possible gamble on peace with Pakistan are worthy of discussion.

First and foremost, India should look beyond getting Pakistan to end cross-border terrorism and explore a final settlement of the Kashmir dispute, without which its war against terrorism would remain unfinished and peace with Pakistan elusive. Moreover, as the shield that had seemingly protected Kashmir from the knuckledusters of global opinion has been pierced irreparably and Kashmir is now out there, on the centrepiece of the agenda on every country that matters, India can no longer continue with business as usual, even if the present stand-off with Pakistan is resolved to India's satisfaction. It is of course a measure of the Vajpayee administration's deep interest in peace that it has not used Pakistan's betrayals at Lahore and Agra to renege on its commitment in this regard. Even in his New Year reflections for the year 2002, the Prime Minister reiterated his commitment to "search for a lasting solution to the Kashmir problem, both in its external and internal dimensions." He has thus shown a rare Indian boldness in taking political risk in dealing with Pakistan. He however now needs to publicly reaffirm this commitment to purposefully address the Kashmir question once Pakistan ends its support to cross border terrorism.

While moving ahead towards this end, the Vajpayee

Government should remember that there is a growing international consensus towards recognising the LoC as the international border, of course, with certain minor adjustments if need be. This consensus was epitomised by the recent comments of Joseph Biden, Chairman of the US Senate Foreign Relations Committee, who asserted, "If India is willing to make substantive changes in its policy towards Kashmir, Pakistan must be wiling to accept the LoC as a border and end its support for insurgency." International consensus apart, there were three occasions when there seemed to have been a near agreement between top Indian and Pakistani leaders that Jammu and Kashmir be partitioned along the Ceasefire Line/LoC.[9] Besides, conversion of LoC into international boundary is the only practical solution, as it is difficult to solve the complex Kashmir problem on the basis of absolutes. Absolute victory is not possible for either India or Pakistan through use of force or diplomacy. Moreover, apart from displacing huge populations, the redrawing of borders in the South Asian, could also lead to huge communal clashes, bloodier than those during the Partition of India. It is also significant to note that the LoC approximately corresponds a broad ethnic-linguistic division within the formerly princely State. Finally, the two parts of Kashmir under Indian and Pakistani control have for more than half century lived as part of India and Pakistan respectively. Although they have grievances against their respective leaderships, there has been a cumulative process of integration that will be extremely difficult to reverse.

Secondly, India should make sure that Musharraf will stand by his promise to end cross-border terrorism and dismantle the "plumbing" in the state structures of Pakistan that supports it on a permanent basis. As Pakistan belied India's expectations at Lahore and Agra that its goodwill and a reasonable approach towards the Kashmir problem might encourage Pakistan to yield on cross-border terrorism, India must not miss the present opportunity provided by the post September 11 global concern against terrorism. Now for the first time since Pakistan adopted cross-border terrorism as an instrument of shaping the process and outcome of dialogue with India in the late 1980s, India has found a way to get it to move in a different direction.

Thirdly, India must keep the international community involved in the process, as without the changed global milieu and Anglo-American pressure, General Musharraf would never have promised to put an end to cross border terrorism. Constant international backing is a must for forcing the General to implement his promise. Since India legs behind Pakistan for the propaganda stakes on the international stage and the recent communal carnage in Gujarat has eroded its image as a tolerant and secular nation,[10] India must vigorously convince the world community that the Kashmir issue, which has a definitive history peculiar to the ethos of India and Pakistan, cannot be equated with Palestine question, which is a basic sense, is related to the political displacement of an entire civil society. True, New Delhi has decided to engage the international community by giving non-polemical diplomacy one more chance at this stage to serve the cause of meaningful restraint maintained by it so far. But fixing the culpability of Pakistan based organization in a reasonably transparent exercise, which places the issue beyond doubt, is necessary to facilitate this. This it not to make light of evidence that new Delhi has already gathered, but only to point towards the need of learning a lesson from the US, which felt compelled, at the height of its anti-terror war in Afghanistan, to release what it classified a providentially obtained video-record. This pertained to Osama bin Laden's confession concerning his role of orchestrating the terrorist offensive against America.

While it is heartening for India that the international community and especially major powers such the US, Britain, Canada, Russia, and Japan, etc., have clearly told Pakistan to stop using terror as a tool of foreign policy, New Delhi should nonetheless impress upon the Bush administration that it is an over simplification on their part to treat both the Vajpayee and Musharraf Governments as victims of terrorism merely because both the countries have experienced terrorist strikes of late. True, for *Al-Qaeda*, Gen Musharraf is as much a foe as the rulers of India and the US, which accounts for several acts of terrorist violence in Pakistan including the recent Karachi blast. But barring *Al-Qaeda*, all terrorist groups in Pakistan continue to enjoy the support and patronage of the Pakistani agencies. If the US is made to grasp this central fact, New Delhi may be able to turn the American "interest" in the sub-continent to its advantage.

Fourthly, gaining from the past experiences, India should prepare well for the next summit with Gen. Musharraf. Part of the failure at Lahore and Agra must be attributed to the desire for quick results from high profile summitry. This time, productive negotiations at the bureaucratic and political levels, as well as through back channels, must precede a decision by Prime Minster, Vajpayee, to travel to Islamabad some time in 2003. Also, the next summit must aim at clinching substantial political understandings, and not merely at initiating a process to arrive a positive outcomes. The Prime Minister must continue to be guided by his grand vision towards Pakistan that took him to Lahore, but that must be supplemented by careful diplomatic preparations this time.

Finally, a national consensus should be built on the strategy of dealing with Pakistan and Kashmir. A special care should be taken not allow the bickering in the Cabinet itself. Several commentators attribute the failure of India's Ramzan peace initiative of November 2000 and the Agra summit of July 2001 to the serious political difference within the Cabinet.[11] Ending this rift is the first step towards building a national consensus on a new political initiative towards Pakistan. As a divided house cannot successfully negotiate peace, India should go for talks with Pakistan with a strong unity and support back at home. It is heartening to note that the major opposition parties have welcomed Vajpyee's recent peace initiative. One can only hope at this juncture that they will continue to maintain this reasonable attitude as the peace process moves ahead.

THE HEALING TOUCH POLICY IN KASHMIR

In the longer-run, however, Pakistan inspired and supported terrorism in the Valley cannot be controlled without the winning the acquiescence, if not the hearts of the people in Kashmir. It is therefore necessary for both the Governments in New Delhi and Srinagar to begin with search for developing a consensus for fulfilling the yearning of the Kashmiris for self-governance and preservation of their special identity, known as Kashmiriat. Unfortunately, the last three Governments in India until recently seemed to have subscribed the view that, with the militancy going into remission and with an elected State Government in place, Kashmir would, like Punjab, return to normal. As is evident, this is not happening after Kargil, as Kashmir is not Punjab. As a substantive initiative, however weary an insistence this may seem, the autonomy issue must now therefore be addressed not just as a ploy, but as a seriously intended praxis.

It is therefore a high time to take a bold initiative towards striking a harmonious balance between the need to integrate Jammu and Kashmir within the national mainstream, and the State's demand for autonomous self-government to make that State as a model for "cooperative federalism." The argument that autonomy for Kashmir will give rise to similar demands from other States and lead to disintegration is a red herring to divert attention from the main issue. No other State signed an Instrument of Accession; J & K was the only State, which acceded to India; other States merged with the Union. When special dispensation was provided for J & K under Article 370, no other State raised objections or sought similar special status.[12] Autonomy for that State, therefore, cannot be equated with any plan for restructuring the Indian federation or for further devolution of powers of the States. Autonomy is needed to change the perception of the Kashmiris that India has gone back to accord special status to the State. This is the least that must be conceded to win back the Kashmiri people, to assuage their hurt feelings and restore their honour and dignity.

It is heartening to note that the India has not only been able to conduct a free and fair elections in that troubles state that brought the present Government led by Mufti Mohammad Sayeed into power there, but also the new Government is sincerely trying to apply healing touch to the ruffled feelings of the Kashmiri peoples. The Government of India on its part has only endorsed this policy of the state Government, but also appointed the former Union Home Secretary, N. N. Vohra, to talk to various sections of peoples to arrive at a consensus towards addressing their problems. Though Hurriyat leaders boycotted the elections as well Vohra mission, but now when the Pakistan Government has partly reciprocated Vajpyee's peace gestures, the Hurriyat leaders too are displaying positive signals for negotiation.

Closely related to the issue of autonomy or self-governance is the desire for good governance. This involves a strong stable economic infrastructure that can unleash the entrepreneurial potential of the people of the State and generate employment; an accountable, streamlined, and people-sensitive administrative machinery; and a speedy grievance redressal system that includes an upright and effective judiciary. As all these are virtually absent in the State through most of this decade. The very fact that Dr. Farooq Abdullah became unpopular despite the popular verdict in his favour in 1996 elections shows that people in Kashmir are yearning not only for self- governance but also for good governance. While Prime Minister, Atal Behari Vajpayee's announcement concerning an economic package of more than 6,000 crore rupees for the development of that State, which he made during his visit to the State in May 2002, is a welcome gesture, ensuring the proper and transparent utilization of this package is more important than the vast amount involved. It is really a welcome sign that Vajpayee has once again promised New Delhi's whole-hearted support to any effort for providing self as well as good governance to the Kashmiri people.

CONCLUSION

India has demonstrated in the past such as after its nuclear tests in 1998 that it has the capability to act as a responsible and mature nation. India as a regional and nuclear power has once again the opportunity to demonstrate its strategic maturity in facing the challenge to its security needs. The terrorism standoff is being forced on India by a Pakistani military leadership, which is itself facing serious difficulties. Strengthening that leadership by a military conflict may prove to be counter-productive for India. New Delhi's capability to counter Pakistan's proxy war against this country will be greatly enhanced by the success of the democratic process in Jammu and Kashmir. It would be essential therefore to increase the range of Indian options rather than narrow them to mere military choices. India's war against Pakistan sponsored terrorism will then be won with the cooperation and support of other nations' war against terrorism instead of opposition to it.

India can succeed in convincing Pakistan about the futility and costs of its anti-India policies, and therefore for converting the LoC into international border only by the three pronged strategy outlined in this paper, namely, defence preparedness, continued mobilization of international support, and winning back the acquiescence of the Kashmiri people. Once India succeeds in this venture, both the neighbours should work towards converting the territory around the LoC into a demilitarised zone. This could contribute to a gradual resumption of trade, free passage of goods, and problem-free travel for people across the border. Peoples living in both sides of the India Pakistan divide could enjoy autonomy in their respective States.

In sum, the climate of opinion, internationally and within Kashmir, offers India an unprecedented opportunity. Rarely, if ever, in the last fifty-five years has there been as real a possibility for finally settling the vexed India-Pakistan dispute over Kashmir as there is today. It would be really a grave tragedy, if this opportunity is squandered because of political inertia or bureaucratic ineptitude.

REFERENCES :

1. This peace initiative was a bold one in the sense that had been seized by India and not by any Pak-sponsored terrorist outfit as was done in July 2000. This shifted the onus of keeping the peace to the warring groups of militants and their mentors across the border. It has also put General Musharraf, already under severe pressure from within his country to restore democracy and slammed for missile exports by the United States, on the defensive.

2. For an analysis of reasons for the failure of the Agra summit, see Nalini Kant Jha, "Southern Asia Internet Forum Dialogue Question XXIII, Part-5, "Life After Agra: What Next?" at *www.stimson.org*

3. In this respect, India acted in accordance with its ancient tradition of exhausting all possible ways of peaceful resolution of conflict. Lord Krishna, for instance, advocated war only after exhausting all possible means of peaceful negotiation of dispute between the Kauravas and the Pandvas. For an elaboration of this point, see Nalini Kant Jha, "Cultural and Philosophical Roots of India's Foreign Policy," *International Studies* (New Delhi), vol. 26, no.1, January-March 1989, pp.45-67.

4. For the text of President General Pervez Musharraf's address to his country on 27th May 2002, see *Strategic Digest* (New Delhi), vol. 32, no.5, May 2002, pp.739-41.

5. For the transcript of the press conference of 28th May 2002 by Shri Jaswant Singh, the then External Affairs Minister, Government of India, see ibid., pp.741-49.

6. Cited by Prem Shankar Jha, "Snap Out of It," *The Hindustan Times* (New Delhi), 5 July 2002.

7. See, for details, "Nalini Kant Jha, "The US, Pokharan-II and South Asia", *India Quarterly* (New Delhi), vol. 55, nos. 1-2, January-June, 1999, pp.1-18; and his, "US-India Relations

after Pokharan-II: Effectiveness of India's Clout", *South Asian Journal of Socio-Political Studies* (Kerala), vol. 1, no. 1, pp. 12-21. Also his, "India and the United States: Pursuit and Limits of Accommodation", *Strategic Analysis* (New Delhi), vol. 27, no. 2, April 1994, pp. 89-107.

8. For an elaboration of this point, see A P Rana, "The Nehruvian Tradition in World Affairs: Its Evolution and Relevance to the Post-Cold War International Relations," in Nalini Kant Jha, ed., *India's Foreign Policy in a Changing World* (New Delhi, 2000), pp.41-46.

9. In 1955, the Prime Minister, Jawaharlal Nehru, and the Pakistani Governor-General, Ghulam Mohammad, are said to have agreed to a divisions along the Ceasefire Line with minor adjustments. Between December 1962 and May 1963, Pakistan's then Foreign Minister, Zulfiqar Ali Bhutto, and Sardar Swaran Singh, a senior Indian Cabinet Minister, discussed a plan for partitioning along the Ceasefire Line. In 1972, Prime Minister, Indira Gandhi, and Z. A Bhutto, too, seemed to have arrived at an understanding that converting the LoC into the international border was the only way out of the Kashmir conundrum.

10. Shishir Gupta, "Upset with Britain and EU, India Charges them with Using Gujarat to Cater to Their Domestic Audiences," *India Today* (New Delhi), vol.27, no.18, 30 April-6 May 2002, pp.42-43.

11. C. Raja Mohan, "Vajpayee: Third Time Lucky?" *The Hindu*, 20 June 2002.

12. Nalini Kant Jha, "Kashmir: Need for a Balanced Peace Initiative", *Journal of Peace Studies* (New Delhi), vol. 7, no. 6, November-December 2000, pp. 37-91. Also his, "Reviving US-India Friendship in a Changing International Order", *Asian Survey* (California, Berkeley), vol. 34, no. 12, 1994, pp. 30-35-46; and N. Krishnan, "Roads that Lead from Kargil", *The Asian Age* (Calcutta), 22 July 1999.

Appendix I

Extracts of : The India Independence Act, July 18, 1947

Be it enacted .... as follows :

I. (1) As from the fifteenth day of August, nineteen hundred and forty seven, two independent Dominions shall be set up in India, to be known respectively as India and Pakistan.

(2) The said Dominions are hereafter in this Act referred to as 'the new Dominions', and the said fifteenth day of August is hereafter in this Act referred to as 'the appointed day'.

II. (1) Subject to the provisions of subsections (3) and (4) of this section, the territories of India shall be the territories under the sovereignty of His Majesty which, immediately before the appointed day, were included in British India except the territories which, under subsection (2) of this section, are to be the territories of Pakistan.

(2) Subject to the provisions of subsections (3) and (4) of this section, the territories of Pakistan shall be –

(a) the territories which, on the appointed day, are included in the Provinces of East Bengal and West Punjab, as constituted under the two following sections;

(b) the territories which, at the date of the passing of this Act, are included in the Province of Sind and the Chief Commissioner's Province of British Baluchistan; and

(c) If, whether before or after the passing of this Act but before the appointed day, the Governor-General declares that the majority of the valid votes cast in the referendum which, at the date of the passing of this Act, is being or has recently been held in that behalf under his authority in the North West Frontier Province are in favour of representatives of that Province taking part in the Constituent Assembly of Pakistan, the territories which at the date of passing of this Act, are included in that Province.

(3) Nothing in this section shall prevent any area being at any time included in or excluded from either of the new Dominions, so however that –

(a) no area not forming part of the territories specified in subsection. (1) or, as the case may be, subsection (2), of this section shall be included in either Dominion without the consent of that Dominion; and

(b) no area which forms part of the territories specified in the said subsection (1) or, as the case may be, the said subsection (2), or which has after the appointed day been included in either Dominion, shall be excluded from that Dominion without the consent of that Dominion.

(4) Without prejudice to the generosity of the provisions of subsection (3) of this section, nothing in this section shall be construed as preventing the accession of Indian States to either of the new Dominions.

III. (1) As from the appointed day –

(a) the Province of Bengal, as constituted under the Government of India Act, 1935, shall cease to exist; and

(b) there shall be constituted in lieu thereof two new Provinces, to be known respectively as East Bengal and West Bengal.

(2) If, whether before or after the passing of this Act, but before the appointed day, the Governor-General declares that the majority of the valid votes cast in the referendum which, at the date of the passing of this Act, is being or has recently been held in that behalf under his authority in the District of Sylhet are in favour of that District forming part of the new province of East Bengal, then, accordance with the provisions of subsection (3) of this section, form part of the new Province of East Bengal.

(3) The boundaries of the new Provinces aforesaid and, in the even mentioned in subsection (2) of this section, the boundaries after the appointed day of the province of Assam, shall be such as may be determined, whether before or after the appointed day, by the award of a boundary commission appointed or to be appointed by the Governor-General in that behalf, but until the boundaries are so determined –

(a) the Bengal Districts specified in the First Schedule to this Act, together with, in the even mentioned in subsection (2) of this section, the Assam District of Sylhet, shall be treated as the territories which are to be comprised in the new Province of East Bengal;

(b) the remainder of the territories comprised at the date of the passing of this Act in the Province of Bengal shall be treated as the territories which are to be comprised in the new Province of West Bengal; and

(c) the event mentioned in subsection (2) of this section, the District of Sylhet shall be excluded from the Province of Assam.

(4) In this section, the expression 'award' means, in relation to a boundary commission, the decisions of the chairman of that commission contained in his report to the Governor-General at the conclusion of the commission's proceedings.

IV. (1) As from the appointed day –

(a) The Province of the Punjab, as constituted under the

Government of India Act, 1935, shall cease to exist; and

(b) there shall be constituted two new Provinces, to be known respectively as West Punjab and East Punjab.

(2) The boundaries of the said new Provinces shall be such as may be determined, whether before or after the appointed day, by the award of a boundary commission appointed or to be appointed by the Governor-General in that behalf, but until the boundaries are so determined –

(a) the Districts specified in the Second Schedule to this Act shall be treated as the territories to be comprised in the new Province of West Punjab; and

(b) the remainder of the territories comprised at the date of the passing of this Act in the Province of the Punjab shall be treated as the territories which are to be comprised in the new Province of the East Punjab.

(3) In this section, the expression 'award' means, in relation to a boundary commission the decisions of the chairman of that commission contained in his report to the Governor-General at the conclusion of the commission's proceedings.

(4) For each of the new Dominions, there shall be a Governor-General who shall be appointed by His Majesty and shall represent His Majesty for the purpose of the government of the Dominion;

Provided, that, unless and until provision to the contrary is made by a law of the Legislature of either of the new Dominions, the same person may be Governor-General of both the new Dominions.

VI. (1) The Legislature of each of the new Dominions shall have full power to make laws for the Dominion, including laws having extra-territorial operation.

(2) No law and no provision of any law made by the Legislature of either of the new Dominions shall be void or inoperative on the ground that it is repugnant to the law of England, or to the provisions

of this or any existing or future Act of Parliament of the United Kingdom, or to any order, rule or regulation made under any such Act, and the powers of the Legislature of each Dominion include the power to repeal or amend any such Act, order, rule or regulation in so far as it is part of the law of the Dominion.

(3) The Governor-General of each of the new Dominions shall have full power to assent in His Majesty's Name to any law of the Legislature of the Dominion and so much of any Act as relates to the disallowance of laws by His Majesty or the reservation of laws for the signification of His Majesty's pleasure thereon or the suspension of the operation of laws the signification of His Majesty's pleasure thereon shall not apply lo laws of the Legislature of either of the new Dominions.

(4) No Act of Parliament of the United Kingdom passed on or after the appointed day shall extend, or be deemed to extend, to either of the new Dominions as part of the law of that Dominion unless it is extended thereto by a law of the Legislature of the Dominion.

(5) No Order in Council made on or after the appointed day under any Act passed before the appointed day, and no order, rule or other instrument made on or after the appointed day under any such Act by any United Kingdom Minister or other authority, shall extend, or be deemed to extend, lo either of the new Dominions as part of the law of that Dominion.

VIII. (1) In the case of each of the new Dominions, the powers of the Legislature of the Dominion shall, for the purpose of making provision as to the constitution of the Dominion, be exercisable in the first instance by the Constituent Assembly of that Dominion, and references in this Act to the Legislature of the Dominion shall be construed accordingly.

(2) Except in so far as other provision is made by or in accordance with a law made by the Constituent Assembly of the Dominion under sub-section (1) of this section, each of the new

Dominions and all Provinces and other parts thereof shall be governed as nearly as may be in accordance with the Government of India Act, 1935 ; and the provisions of that Act, and the Orders in Council, rules and other instruments made thereunder, shall, so far as applicable, and subject to any express provisions of this Act, and with such omissions, additions, adaptations and modifications as may be specified in orders of the governor-General.

XI. (1) The orders to be made by the Governor-General under the preceding provisions of this Act shall make provision for the division of the Indian Armed Forces of His Majesty between the new Dominions, and for the command and governance of those forces until the division is completed.

(2) As from the appointed day, while any member of His Majesty's forces, other than His Majesty's Indian forces, is attached to or serving with any of His Majesty's Indian forces —

(a) he shall, subject to any provision to the contrary made by a law of the Legislature of the Dominion or Dominions concerned or by any order of the Governor-General under the preceding provisions of this Act, have, in relation to the Indian forces in question, the powers of command and punishment appropriate lo his rank and functions ; but

(b) nothing in any enactment in force at the date of the passing of this Act shall render him subject in any way to the law governing the Indian forces in question.

XVIII. (3) Save as otherwise expressly provided in this Act, the law of British India and of the several parts thereof existing immediately before the appointed day shall, so far as applicable and with the necessary adoptions, continue as the law of each of the new Dominions and the several parts thereof until other provision is made by law of the Legislature of the Dominions in question or by any other Legislature or other authority having power in that behalf.

XX. This Act may be cited as the Indian Independence Act, 1947.

APPENDIX V

Text of the Clinton-Sharif Statement, July 5, 1999

President Clinton and Prime Minister Sharif share the view that the current fighting in the Kargil region of Kashmir is dangerous and contains the seeds of a wider conflict. They also agreed that it was vital for the peace of South Asia that the Line of Control in Kashmir be respected by both parties, in accordance with the 1972 Simla accord.

It was agreed between the President and the Prime Minister that concrete steps will be taken for the restoration of the Line of Control in accordance with the Simla Agreement. The President urged an immediate cessation of the hostilities once these steps are taken.

The Prime Minister and President agreed that the bilateral dialogue begun in Lahore in February provides the best forum for resolving all issues dividing India and Pakistan, including Kashmir. The President said he would take a personal interest in encouraging an expeditious resumption and intensification of those bilateral efforts, once the sanctity of the Line of Control has been fully restored.

The President reaffirmed his intent to pay an early visit to South Asia.

Source: *The Hindu*, 6 July 1999.

Index